MW01233277

IN THE ARENA

Saumita Banerjee

Jean-Marie Buchilly

Yehoshua Zlotogorski

Simon Krystman

Shyjal Raazi

Aluwani Nemukula

Aditya Bhatnagar

Susanna Nissar

Christopher Norris

Donal O'Connell

Massimo Scalzo

Meenakshi Babu

Ilanit Appelfeld

Susanna Schumacher

Suraj Rajan

First Printing: 2021

Hardcover ISBN: 978-81-952590-1-4
Paperback: 978-81-952590-2-1
Ebook: 978-81-952590-3-8

Illustrations by SCAPH
Typeset by Ram Das Lal
Edited by Jyotirmoy Chaudhuri

LetsAuthor
www.letsauthor.com

Everything you're striving for is a by-product of something else—
something bigger.

Innovation is a by-product of empathy.

Winning ideas are a by-product of taking risks.

Excellence is the by-product of empowered cultures.

Profits are the by-product of happy customers.

Success is a by-product of mattering.

— BERNADETTE JIWA,
in Meaningful, The Story of Ideas That Fly

WHY THIS BOOK IS RIGHT FOR YOU

"Everyone is a genius at least once a year. The real geniuses simply have their bright ideas closer together."

– Georg Christoph Lichtenberg,
18th-century German philosopher and physicist

Great ideas occur quite often. We encounter problems all the time, and in many instances come up with smart, innovative ideas to solve them. However, we seldom do anything more with such ideas. The world is full of incredible ideas that never go anywhere because great ideas are useless unless someone implements them.

If you have an idea that is close to your heart or are aware of a problem you desperately want to solve, then this book is for you. It is designed to steer you toward deciding and implementing your big idea. You may be an entrepreneur, a teacher, an employee, a housewife, or a social activist. No matter what you are today, if you have the slightest of intent to work upon your idea, we believe you will find this book helpful in making your idea a reality.

It is not a book you read in a day, but rather a prescriptive manual you keep with you and consult from time to time. It will help you think through your idea and transform it into an innovative and successful product or solution.

Whether you want to start a business, create a regular source of income in addition to your job, build a financial backup, or just experience the thrill of making your idea happen, this book is for you.

If your idea can jumpstart with bootstrapped money and self-sustain within a short time, this book is for you. However, if your idea needs huge investments to crank up—one with high monetary barriers, you may still find this book useful. It will guide you in validating your idea, and help you nurture it into a more concrete form before you present it to an investor, increasing your chances of success getting your first big funding.

Most breakthrough ideas emerge out of serendipity—when you are not looking for them. Such ideas have the potential to become disruptive innovations and are found to be more powerful than the ones that come out of an active search. They have the power to change the world, to bring about those 'tipping point' moments that propel the world into a different trajectory. This book is about nurturing new ideas and helping you build a company that creates new things. Ideas that take the world from "zero to one."[1]

Funding and abundance are not the holy grail to success. Constraints breed creativity. You will learn to be creative with the resources you have at your disposal and make the best use of them, with minimum wastage and maximum learning.

This book is for:

1. Enterprising individuals with new ideas.
2. "Wannabe" entrepreneurs.
3. Struggling entrepreneurs.
4. Founders/co-founders of prelaunch or early-stage startups.
5. Corporate employees with intrapreneurial ambitions: executives, product managers, designers, developers, marketers, analysts.

David Hieatt, Co-founder, Hiut Denim Co. and author of *Do Purpose: Why brands with a purpose do better and matter more* writes, "Great ideas often have no reference points. We have nothing to compare them to. They are original, and awkward. And so they are the most vulnerable to people trying to kill them. They do not conform to what exists, so they challenge us."[2]

Ideas do not care about who you are and what you do for a living. All that matters is that the idea came to you, and it matters to the world. Now it's your duty to cultivate and transform it into an innovation. Act toward bringing the change you want to see. This book is written to help you take action.

Contents

III: STEP INTO THE ARENA

IV: SHOW YOURSELF

V: SUSTAIN AND THRIVE

THE STORY OF THIS BOOK

"I'm thinking of writing a book on innovation, but I don't have the time to write the entire book all by myself." These words, spoken by Andy Zynga, Ph.D., a practitioner in the Innovation Management space, spurred the beginning of a revolution in the world of book writing. Andy said this to me, then a Technology Analyst at NineSigma, the company Andy was CEO of at the time.

The need Andy articulated back then was, and still is, a real one. Each one of us, in the course of our personal and professional lives, has accumulated vast amounts of knowledge and experience. Many of us want to share with the world all that we have learned—what worked for us, what didn't, what we could have done better, the lessons we learned in the process, and so on. Some of you might share such knowledge through blogs, articles, and posts. But not all of us have the inclination, the time, and sometimes the talent, to put it all together in the form of a book. However, the prospect of having your own published book can be quite enticing. From the earliest scrolls and parchments to the new-age e-books, books have a timeless feel about them. Any one of you may have read so many books that have collectively contributed to a major part of all that you know today. Blogs and articles often don't have the kind of impact that a book might have on our minds.

So, after Andy had stated his need for help with that book on innovation, he and I started brainstorming on how to make that happen without having to commit too much of our time and effort. We decided that the best way would be to divide the burden among many in the tradition of Open Innovation. We both worked at Open Innovation pioneer NineSigma at the time and using a tool such as crowdsourcing wasn't so far from our knitting, to begin with. What, if we were to create a community and ask it to come together and write the book in a joint effort? What, if we were to structure the book around a few chapters, and solicit the community's help to populate the chapters? And, instead of just acknowledging their contributions, make them a stakeholder in the project—designate them as co-authors and share royalties from the book with them? This approach could make the process of writing books much simpler and quicker. It also had the potential to generate healthy social interactions within the co-author teams.

The idea was brilliant, but then, life happened. We both got busy with our respective work and the idea remained an idea. For a long time—about nine months. In March 2019, I made a new friend who happened to have a website development background. The book writing idea, that was still latent in my mind, sprung up to life. I shared my book idea with her and took the first tangible step toward executing the thought that was until then only in my head. From then on, my life changed.

All my life I had worked on executing others' ideas. Solving problems that came from someone else. As employees, we work on a project that is given to us as part of the job. Solving a *client's* problem, developing codes, manufacturing, marketing, or selling our *company's* products. Think about it, when was the last time you did something that originated from you? What, if you could devote all your talent and energy to working on *that* idea?

For me, for the first time, the problem I was about to work on was identified by me (well, Andy and me), and the idea was conceived by us. You cannot imagine the sense of ownership until you start working on your unique idea! It was as if something shifted inside. Sure, there was a lot more responsibility, a lot of uncertainty, and confusion, but the kind of passion and freedom it brought was unparalleled. I felt alive, more involved. There is a reason why we love our children so much. Motherhood and fatherhood are, I think, an embodiment of this sense of ownership.

Thus began the journey of "LetsAuthor," the publishing startup that has made this book happen. I don't have a business background, but a technical one. I had never planned or professionally prepared myself to become an entrepreneur. But once I stumbled upon my big idea, it pulled me into this whole new world beyond the realm of technical knowledge. I figured how to incorporate a company, find and hire the right professionals, manage funding and finances, set the rules for the platform, understand the legal implications, manage compliance, and so on.

It's been humbling and at the same time, liberating. Humbling because I knew that I was starting from zero, I was aware that I didn't know so much, and was learning. The ego component was reduced substantially. Liberating because I was not tethered to any idea or ideology, I was free of the burden of knowledge of the industry. It was like being a child again, but without the overseeing eyes of a parent. I could do anything I wanted; the implications rested only with me. If I worked smartly, I got to reap the benefits. If I acted dumb, I was the one to suffer the implications. Which was fine. There was no performance pressure.

Several months and a change of vendor later, a version of the digital platform was finally ready to be opened to the public. I wish I had had this book to read before we started building the LetsAuthor platform. When we first started, I had a vague idea about what the platform will look like, based on other writing platforms—Wikipedia and WattPad being the most relevant ones—and we started from there. Without a clear understanding of what features might be the most important to *our* platform, we worked simultaneously into developing multiple features. Apart from the basic collaborative writing functionality, we worked on several other features that I now realize are important, but secondary. We spent time designing an author community framework, author profile pages, commenting features, and so on. This made the platform too complex. Costs mounted, timelines stretched, seemingly indefinitely. It looked like the platform would never take off. I might have needed to abandon the project.

But I persisted. I had to. I relooked at the whole thing with a fresh new perspective. I realized that we were trying to achieve too much. We needed to simplify things. We identified elements that were bare essential to test and validate the concept of Open Authoring and shaved off all secondary features. We focused only on refining the core features. This was our Minimum Viable Product—our MVP. And we finally launched this MVP in November 2020. The first book we opened on the platform, to be written through Open Authoring, is the very book you are holding in your hands right now. This book you are about to read was not written by one single expert. It was written by fifteen co-authors, each directly associated with the entrepreneurial world. Through this book, they offer you their collective wisdom on how to cultivate your big idea and make it a reality. I will forever be indebted to all co-authors who became a part of this book, the early adopters, who supported the vision and agreed to share their knowledge and experiences. Early adopters are the lifeline of any startup.

The platform is still an MVP. There is so much more to do to bring Open Authoring to the mainstream. To fulfill the vision of a platform that enables everyone to share with the world their unique experiences and knowledge, in whatever field they are passionate about, through their own published books. While working on this book, I have learned, as an entrepreneur, some important lessons that I intend to utilize in my journey from an MVP to a mainstream product.

The majority of us are the players, and only a few make the actual rules of the game. Playing can be fun but getting to make the rules is far more empowering.

It all starts with your idea. If it's your idea, you get to make the rules. But then the question is, how to make the rules so that the game is engaging and entertaining? You may have the authority, but unless you make something that the players find interesting, no one will play your game.

The success of your idea lies in its ability to positively affect the lives of those using it. The greater the number of people it can affect, the more successful your idea will be! The magic lies in the idea itself, which has the potential to transform the lives of those you seek to serve. It is not about you; it is about them.

Through my idea, I seek to change the way great books are written. What is the change you are seeking? Don't hesitate, and don't rush it. Have patience. Your idea will see the light of day if you persist. But your journey will not end there. You will need to persevere, each day, and continuously test, validate, and optimize your product, your business, your life. The immense satisfaction you will get and the things you will learn in the process will be your greatest reward. Use this book to navigate through your journey, but remember, the journey is yours to make.

— *Saumita Banerjee*
Bengaluru, June 2021

INTRODUCTION

Every innovative business starts with a vision and an idea. Steve Jobs' vision was of a "computer for the rest of us." Computers around that time were far too complicated, and out of the price range of an average individual. Steve's idea was to simplify computers, making them easy to use, intuitive and affordable. To change the status quo and give the individual the same power as any company. Mark Zuckerberg started Facebook with a vision of a more open world. Mark's idea was to give people a tool to share the information they wanted and have access to the information they wanted.

The ideas Jobs and Zuckerberg came up with are not uncommon. We humans can think, and by thinking we keep coming up with ideas to solve problems. Indeed, the propensity to solve problems is hard-wired into our very system. Creative problem-solving "lights up" the brain's reward system, releasing the mood-enhancing chemical dopamine: that is when you experience your *Aha! moment*.[3]

Most ideas originate from problems we face in our daily lives (some ideas may originate from loftier goals—Elon Musk's passion for space transportation, and his massive battery "gigafactory"—but let's not venture into that direction). For example, I'm craving to eat something delicious, but do not intend to make it myself, or go out and eat. So, what do I do? In an era before online food ordering, the idea of one-click food ordering and home delivery may have occurred to many, but only a few had the conviction to go ahead with the idea, work out the practicalities of executing it, and start up a business catering to this peculiar need. Some of these entrepreneurial individuals are today heading unicorn startups—India's Swiggy is one such shining example.

If you have had your *Aha! moment*, and want to do something with it, we wrote this book for you. Through this book, you will get to know the single most important thing that will make your idea fly. You will learn to nurture your initial idea—the raw, "uncooked" version—into an innovation, a solution that

- your customer desires and will pay for,
- is workable for you within your constraints and capabilities, and
- is viable—something from which you can make money and continue serving your customers.

Every innovation is unique, but the journey from an idea to an innovation can fit within a common framework. You can find value in unexpected places, but identifying the value at the right time, and systematically working toward increasing that value is all about being innovative. As Peter Thiel says in his book *Zero to One*, copying an existing model is far easier than creating something new. But copying only adds to competition, and competition is a "margin-eater." If you have an idea that promises to create something new, you have the potential to open up a "blue ocean"—a new market space—and create new demand.

The path to failure is the one without any action. If you do not act, you have already failed in achieving your goal. But there is time, and there are loads of activities you can do to change course—to move away from failure and toward success.

This is not luck, if you succeed, you don't want to be one of those "lucky" ones. You will have done it through a structured approach, by systematically evaluating every single thing you are doing, and systematically finding the things that will steer you sharply toward success. By engineering your success through well-designed experiments.

So, crank up the engine, and be ready to steer. Because, unless you take the car out of the garage, you will never reach your destination. Get ready to take on the wheels, because if you don't, you will never get to drive it in the direction you want.

Start with identifying a problem worth solving. A problem big enough or a solution attractive enough that will make people pull out money from their pockets. And then engineer the best solution that will stir them to part with their money. To know what will excite them, you present the solution to them and experiment with the items and features that hold their attention. No speculations, no guesses, no whiteboard strategizing, only real customer feedback.

It generally happens that we start with a spark, an idea, and then we get passionate about it, see ourselves through it, our success through it. It becomes our identity. Do not identify yourself with your idea. Because it may not be the best one out there. Keep yourself emotionally distanced from your idea and try to "kill your darlings." There are so many unknowns in deciding if your idea is the best or not. Go out and first check if the problem you are out to solve is big enough to warrant any effort at all. If it isn't, no one will care about your idea and your product. If the problem is big enough, then validate if your idea indeed is the best. What is best after all? Best is relative. It is relative to what other solutions are out there, and who is using them, and for what purpose. So many factors. So subjective.

When you have distanced yourself from your initial idea, you will be open to changing its nuances, or even abandoning it altogether and finding another one. You will not be tied to it; you will be free. You will be able to look at it as a set of experiments.

The key to success is to selflessly take on the problem at hand and solve it objectively. The moment you start thinking about the profits you will gain from the activity you begin to crowd your mind with fear and stress. When you selflessly work toward your goal of affecting someone else's life, you get to put all your attention to that task, and then the task is accomplished in the most exquisite manner. Success comes as a by-product.

The cornerstone of everything you do, no matter what perspective you look at it from—spirituality, philosophy, or business—is EMPATHY.

When you look at the problem from the perspective of those you want to serve, get into their shoes and then think about a solution—of how the solution can help them (again, empathy)—you come up with a truly useful solution, and that translates into your success.

Put your complete attention to what you are doing and remember why you are doing it—the change you are trying to bring, your purpose. Your ultimate benefit is about succeeding in bringing about that change. When you place yourself aside from the problem at hand, you get to solve the problem with love. And that love, though intangible to the senses, can be felt. It affects the emotional part of your customer's brain. They feel for you, for your product, and they make decisions they *feel* are right.

Every idea deserves the opportunity to be evaluated for its innovation potential and brought to life. Innovation is the reason people prosper and is the sole contributor to raising living standards. We cannot afford to let go of great ideas that may alter the lives of people and perhaps change the very structure of our society in the times to come. This book aims to empower you, the idea originator, with the knowledge to nurture your ideas into innovative, successful businesses, no matter *where* you are located and *what* resources you have at your disposal.

Trying to turn our ideas into reality and contribute to a better world is not a right but a duty that we all have in a society undergoing profound change. Deciding to play is not enough. Criticizing the rules of the game while continuing to play is even less so. Credit goes to those who change the rules of the game to make it even more exciting. We are sure that you have the desire and the capacity to change these rules. Through this book, we want to help you take action.

I

YOUR BRILLIANT IDEA

1
YOUR SERENDIPITOUS DISCOVERY

It was the year 2006. Melanie, a 19-year-old undergraduate from a university in Perth, on Australia's west coast, was working as a part-timer, teaching fellow students how to use computer programs to design posters, flyers, and school yearbooks. The programs were so hard to learn that "people would have to spend an entire semester learning where the buttons were, and that seemed completely ridiculous." She observed this problem for some time, and thought, why do things have to be so cumbersome in the age of the internet? Why can't there be a simpler solution to do it all in one place with one online tool?

She thought of an idea of a web platform to make the designing process very simple. So simple that anyone without the least exposure to design software could do it all on their own. The problem felt so pressing and obvious that she feared someone else might build a solution if she delayed. She began working on a war footing. She narrowed her focus to one niche market—school yearbooks, hired freelancers to build a Flash website to cater to this market, and launched her startup Fusion Books along with her boyfriend Cliff. She was so convinced and passionate about her idea that with one semester of college left, she put her studies on pause and focused her attention on her startup. Her mother's living room became their office, they worked the phones cold-calling prospects, printed the yearbooks, and delivered them to schools across Australia. They were enabling schools to create their yearbooks really, really simply.[4]

The business was a resounding success. But for Melanie, it was only a start. Her dream was "crazy, big," it was of a one-stop-shop design site to create anything and everything visually appealing: social media graphics, presentations, posters, greeting cards, and so on. Six years, consistent "no" from over a hundred investors, and a kitesurfing training later, she had her first funding round of $1.5 million. Thus began the story of Canva, the global design juggernaut that is valued at over $15 billion (as of April 2021). Over 55 million active users from 190 countries use Canva's "freemium" model to design everything from catchy Instagram graphics to tasteful restaurant menus. Melanie and Cliff, who married in January 2021, each own about 15 percent stake in Canva, and according to *Forbes*, the power couple is worth $4 billion.[5]

According to Miguel Aubouy,[6] a Canadian French-speaking author, innovation thinker, and entrepreneur with a philosophical approach to innovation, a universal innovation process is as simple as three steps:

1. Key observation—you observe something that doesn't work or can be made better.

2. Key idea—you find a solution to the key observation.

3. Key object—you create the first version of a prototype to show that your key idea solves the key observation.

Before the key observation, the process is chaotic and random. You are not expecting a key observation; it just happens. The attributes of a key observation, according to Aubouy, are the facts that it is *detailed, singular, obvious* but *elusive.*

At the moment of the key observation, you do not know that it's a key observation. You only observed something that doesn't work. Or something that can improve.

The key observation is just an observation. Nothing happens until we take the second step: form a key idea.

The key idea is the idea that connects with the key observation and has the potential to improve or solve it.

So, you see, the key idea does not come out of nowhere; you had the key observation somewhere in your head already. But it is certainly linked to serendipity as until then the key observation did not occupy your conscious mind. You did not obsess over it. In fact, the key observation becomes a key observation at the moment the key idea happens.

This process is impromptu and often a happy chance. It didn't come to you from organized thinking. You happened to have the key observation, and subsequently "stumbled" upon the key idea. Almost as if destiny had it planned for you. It feels good to think that way, doesn't it? As Dr. Albert Szent-Gyorgyi, the 1937 Nobel Prize Winner in Physiology or Medicine said in what is now an oft-quoted aphorism: *"Discovery is seeing what everybody else has seen and thinking what nobody else has thought."*

It is possible to reduce the chaos and inject some "organization and focus" in the system by actively searching for a key observation (focusing your attention on a field and looking for the specific pain points to solve) and a key idea (organizing specific activities around the key observation and using methodologies and tools to look for a potential solution). That is what organizations do when they innovate. They do it because their vision and strategy are already in place and there is a real benefit for them to innovate in a controlled framework (field and timeframe). As a kind of trade-off, what we gain here in terms of focus, timeline, and determination, we probably lose in terms of pure creativity in innovation. What will come out of a "controlled process" is likely closer to continuous improvement or incremental innovation than disruptive innovation.

Since you have picked this book to read, the chances are that you already have a key idea to a key observation. Now revisit your key idea and observe it from this new standpoint. How did you come across your idea? Was it a result of serendipity? Or did you arrive at it through a controlled process? Please do not judge, but only observe.

From the moment of your key idea coming into shape, the process follows a different dynamic. You are now looking for something. And this something is the third element of the process: a key object—proof that your idea works.

Building a key object is different from making a key observation or forming a key idea. It is about prototyping and making the idea a reality. It's the longest part of the process and the one that requires the most discipline and perseverance. James Dyson, the legendary British inventor entrepreneur, when designing "the vacuum cleaner without a bag," built no less than 5,127 prototypes before reaching the final version of what has become a successful innovation.[7]

So, when does your idea become an innovation?

It is a question of scale, according to Aubouy. An idea or

invention happens at a "micro" level. At the very beginning, it's one person who has the key idea. Some people transform it into a key object, which is an invention, through a process. However, it's not an innovation—yet.

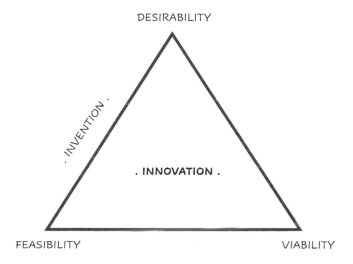

Figure 1: When does your idea become an innovation? It is a question of scale. When considering the design thinking triangle, an invention corresponds to solving the desirability–feasibility equation, as innovation solves the full triangle. An innovation is an invention with commercial and business traction.

It will become an innovation once it gains traction and reaches the "macro" level. It's an invention with commercial and business traction.

When considering the famous design thinking triangle: desirability–feasibility–viability, an invention corresponds to solving the desirability–feasibility equation as the innovation solves the full triangle.

(*Jean-Marie Buchilly* and *Saumita Banerjee*)

2
WHY THIS IDEA?

Simon Sinek, in his book, *Start with Why*,[8] elegantly describes the one thing that differentiates an innovative company and inspiring leadership from one that is based on manipulating customers to act. He describes the concept of the Golden Circle, a perspective to explain why some companies, Apple Inc being a prime example, exert so much influence over their customer base. He asserts that it all starts with WHY.

Most ventures begin by first defining WHAT products or services they want to develop and then HOW they would do it. That sounds about right, doesn't it? But there is one missing detail: WHY do you care to do it? You may say that I want to do it to make money, make profits. I want to start something of my own, become self-reliant, and do away with someone else telling me what to do. These are all valid reasons, but they don't define your WHY.

Your WHY is closely linked to your purpose, cause, or belief. Why do you care? What is it in the idea that is fueling your passion to make this happen? What lights your flame and motivates you? What change do you wish to see? Why is that important to you?

What unique skills or assets do you have at your disposal that make you capable of solving this problem?

The Golden Circle starts with the WHY at the center. When you place your WHY at the center of everything you do, you gain clarity. You devote yourself to building something bigger than you—to a *higher purpose*. You inspire your customers, appealing to their emotional side. You sound more authentic (because you *are* being more authentic). You drive their behavior beyond an analytical, rational understanding of the features of your product. Connecting with your company *feels* right.

Apple's WHY has been to change the status quo and empower individuals with simpler, easier-to-use alternatives to existing solutions. The company did not limit its WHY to a specific product or industry. They were not just a computer business. Apple started with personal computers but went on to disrupt the music industry with the iPod; the mobile phone, telecom, and gaming industries with the iPhone; and are leaving their mark on industries as diverse as healthcare (Apple Watch), television and entertainment (Apple TV), and smart homes. Their customers identify themselves with Apple's products. Apple, it seems, has a very clear picture of who its customers are, and appeals to the status, worldviews, and beliefs of those customers. We'll talk more about status, worldviews, and beliefs in Chapter 5.

The three tiers of Sinek's Golden Circle closely resemble the three steps of Aubouy's universal innovation process. The key observation—the status quo that you want to change—is your WHY. The key idea is HOW you will make the change happen. And the key object is your WHAT—your product.

When you closely and deeply tie your key observation to the needs of your customer, you embark on a journey to make your idea an innovation. You may be passionate about building something, bringing about a change, shifting the status quo, but it is important to understand who it is valuable for, apart from you? Placing your customer at the center—the WHO—an adapted version of the Golden Circle will look like this:

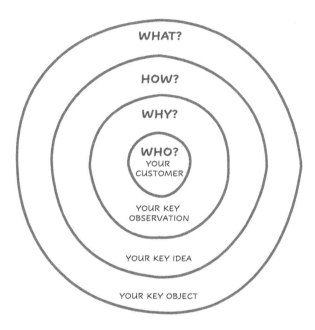

Figure 2: The three tiers of Simon Sinek's Golden Circle (adapted here) closely resemble the three steps of Miguel Aubouy's universal innovation process. The key observation, your WHY, is the status quo that you want to change. The key idea is HOW you will make it happen. The key object is your WHAT, your product. Your customer, the WHO is at the center so that you are clear who your product is valuable for, apart from yourself.

Entrepreneurial spirits have loads of ideas, which is not just great, but essential for business growth and development. Make sure you press the buttons for that one idea that truly engages you, in that you find absolute interest. Great business ideas won't be great unless someone makes them a reality. Think of your presumptive business as your new partner. Ask yourself: "Why is this idea the one I want to give all my attention and resources to? Live, laugh, cry, and still get out of bed every morning with?" Constantly be in touch with and remind yourself about your WHY.

Start your new venture with your WHY articulated, and always with your WHO in mind. You will build a more meaningful business. You will not worry about how to differentiate your products in the market. Your product will not be a commodity, and your customers will know that. You will offer them way more value, and you will not have to convince them. Making decisions at every step of your business will be far easier, and you will operate from a more authentic standpoint. You will inspire yourself and others around you.

(*Saumita Banerjee* and *Susanna Schumacher*)

II

THE GROUNDWORK

3
EMBRACE THE UNCERTAINTY AND MAKE BETTER DECISIONS

As an entrepreneur, you will realize that in everything you do, in every decision you make, there is always an element of uncertainty. There is uncertainty in the people, in the technology, in the product, in the market. Ideas, inventions, and innovations have to be allowed to grow in their distinctive crucibles if they are to be transformed into commercial success. This is a long journey made up of several decisions. Making decisions will be one of your complex responsibilities every day. This will not be easy. Especially because you will never have all the data.

In such a case, you would be tempted to postpone your decision. Unfortunately, this is not possible. Because deciding to postpone a decision is a decision in itself.

To cut a long story short, you cannot avoid making decisions even when data is lacking. Fortunately, making decisions is partly a skill, and you can learn it. The Decision Maker's Canvas is a handy tool to use when making decisions. It can be applied to any decision you make—in business or in everyday life—to make structured, systematic decisions instead of random, irrational, or impulsive ones. The framework is described in terms of the jobs you will perform as a decision-maker.

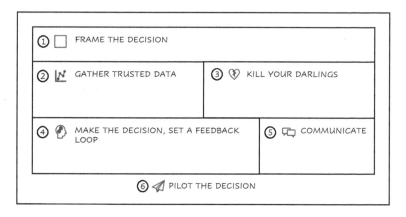

Figure 3: Use the Decision Maker's Canvas to make structured, systematic decisions instead of random, irrational, or impulsive ones. The framework is described in terms of the jobs you will perform as a decision-maker.

First job of the decision-maker: frame the decision correctly

Framing your decision is an essential part of the decision-making process.[9] Start by defining the question on which you have to make your decision. Once you define the question perfectly, the answer flows almost by itself.

There are some framing possibilities that can interfere with and affect the quality of your decision. Check your framing for these possibilities.

Making a gain or avoiding a loss?

There will be an inherent cognitive bias in your decision-making on whether you present your options with positive or negative connotations, for example, as a loss or as a gain. A positive framing focuses on the gain you can make. A negative framing focuses on the loss you can avoid. Always remember that we value our potential losses twice as much as our potential gains. Sunk cost is an example of this phenomenon.[10]

When the supersonic plane Concorde was being built, the costs rose higher than anticipated during the early stages of development. Though the financial success became unclear, the decision-makers went on funding the project because of the money they had already invested.[11] They persisted with the investment and resisted change to another, suitable option keeping in mind the sunk cost from the investment already made.

In the game of poker, when an average player is losing, they tend to play again and again, with the goal of recovering the money they lost. They persist only because they have lost the previous ones. That's anything but a good reason to continue the game. The main decision element being used here is the sunk cost. The quality of their poker hand comes second. An aberrant way to make a decision.

Can I widen the scope?

If you have set a frame that is much too narrow when defining your question, the quality of your decision would benefit from widening your scope of reflection. Consider the framing of the following questions:

1. How do we safely dispose of the nuclear waste being produced?

2. Given our system for energy distribution and consumption, how should we produce energy? Should we produce it in

a way that leads to the generation of additional nuclear waste?[12]

In the first question, we limit our scope to deciding on ways to safely dispose of nuclear waste, whereas in the second question, we have widened the scope of our decision-making by giving ourselves the chance to decide whether we should use the nuclear route at all.

If you are to decide between choosing company A or company B to acquire in order to grow, widening the scope of your decision-making will mean that you stop and think whether company acquisition is the only route to growth? What are your other options? Veteran marketer and nonprofit professional Katya Andresen says, "The question often should not be 'whether or not,' but 'what else?' or maybe even 'what if?' "[13]

Did I define my constraints correctly?

Constraints can counterintuitively boost creativity. It's not rare to get better alternatives when constraining the frame of the decision. Constraints can be beautiful as asserted in Adam Morgan and Mark Barden's exceptional book on the topic.[14] We live in a world full of constraints, driven as much by scarcity of time and resources as by an overabundance of choices. When we move beyond the "victim" stage, we can see the underlying opportunities better and transform ourselves and our organization's fortunes. Identify and put the most pressing constraints at the heart of your process, focus on "how," not "if," and transform your constraints into opportunities.

Am I making a decision under "pressure"?

Remember the Challenger space shuttle explosion? On January

28, 1986, the Challenger exploded 73 seconds after liftoff, killing seven crew members and sending shockwaves through manned spaceflight that remains to the day. The cause of the disaster was traced to an "O-ring," a gasket that sealed the right rocket booster. It had failed because of the low temperature (31°F/-0.5°C) during the time of launch. Although some unfavorable data were flagged, a decision was made to maintain the launch. It was made during a round table. Some decision-makers had earlier decided to postpone the launch, thinking about the best and safest solution. They nevertheless voted the opposite under the "pressure" of the people who preceded them and who had decided to maintain the launch.[15] The social and hierarchical context in which decisions are made can have a powerful effect. Most of us are not very comfortable defending an opinion that goes against the majority or the authority. The quality of the decisions we make is much better in a sheltered place.[16]

Second job of the decision-maker: gather trusted data and define a model

To make a quality decision, even when some data are not available, you need to still collect what is at hand. Because you cannot access the complete information does not mean that you let go of what is available. In the case of the Challenger event, the decision-makers clearly had some unfavorable data but did not consider it when deciding to go ahead with the launch.[17]

We are biased, and we focus on the information that confirms our beliefs instead of looking for trusted sources. Beware of this tendency and pick only data that comes from reliable sources: individuals, communities, or organizations who have legitimacy in the field in which the decision has to be made. It's not the last who spoke who is right. Not all opinions and assertions have the same value.

To make the situation even more difficult, we tend to focus on "the tip of the iceberg." The iceberg is the whole situation, the holistic perspective. The tip of the iceberg is where all eyes are focused. Usually, it's the falsely and easily understandable part of the problem. By mistakenly defining the frame of the decision and considering only the tip instead of the whole iceberg, we end up making decisions that are not very robust on a long-term basis. Because the point at which our eyes are focused can change quickly. And once it does, the decision we made does not make so much sense.

Take the Covid-19 pandemic as an example. We are only considering (and reacting to) the tip of the iceberg, which are Covid-19's direct effects and impacts on physical health. We do not consider the submerged part of this same iceberg which are the indirect effects and impacts of Covid-19—the ones induced by the decisions and measures taken—and the consequences at a global level including all the elements of our society; the social, the mental, and the economic.

The different layers—health, economy, and social—are not successive but interconnected and interpenetrated. We cannot think in silos and take a "health-only" approach first, then decide to switch to the economy, and finally consider the social aspects. The multiple components of the problem are indivisible; they have to be considered as a whole.

Once you have gathered all data available, define a model. A model is not the reality, but it helps us structure and organize our thinking.[18]

The traditional way to decide between two options is to consider the decision-making process as an optimization problem and find a trade-off between option A and option B: the solution we can live with—the compromise.

It is possible to move beyond trade-offs. "Integrative thinking" offers an alternative, more ambitious way to build models as described by Jennifer Riel and Roger L. Martin in their book *Creating Great Choices*.[19] According to Riel and Martin, integrative thinking is:

> ... the ability to face constructively the tensions of opposing models, and instead of choosing one at the expense of the other, generating a creative resolution of the tension in the form of a new model that contains elements of the individual models, but is superior to each.

It means taking the best of choices A and B and creatively reconfiguring them to create new value.

Riel and Martin provide a simple and actionable four-step process:

1. **Articulate the models**: Understand the problem (typically a "How might we ...?" question) and opposing models (your options) more deeply. Typical opposing models are short term versus long term, customization versus standardization, or even local versus global, to mention just a few. A pro–pro chart, highlighting only the benefits of each opposing model, is a great opportunity to show that both models represent opportunities and that a powerful combination is worth designing.

2. **Examine the models**: Define the points of tension,[20]

21

assumptions, and cause-and-effect forces. Reframe if you find a more meaningful problem to solve.

3. **Explore the possibilities**: Play with the pathways to integration. Combine the best part of each model and throw everything else away ("The Hidden Gem"), add a single key element of one model to the other one ("The Double Down"), or use each model to solve different parts of the problem ("Decomposition") to generate possibilities.

4. **Assess the prototypes**: Test and refine the possibilities. Make abstract ideas concrete through storytelling, visualization, and physical modeling. Shift your mindset from thinking to doing with an eye toward gathering new data about the world.

Build a model to gain a holistic and long-term view of the situation, using available and trusted information or data. Put your stories and assertions in perspective in order to transform your opinions into more solid statements. Do not immediately make decisions or act on your ideas or on what you have heard or read in the last article but use these elements to build a holistic vision of the situation and make the most informed decision, supported by solid facts.

To consider the whole iceberg and not only the tip is very hard. And this directly brings us to the human side of the decision-making process. This is the third job of the decision-maker.

Third job of the decision-maker: kill your darlings and neutralize your ego

Making good decisions requires that we kill at the same time our darlings and neutralize our egos, which are two very strong filters that prevent us from seeing the reality as (close as) it is.

We all have beliefs that help us in framing our worldview. Our worldview is subjective and does not reflect the reality.[21] Knowing this is a great first step. The second one is to consider other worldviews. Those that are close and complementary and even those that are opposite. In fact, we cannot get entirely rid of our worldview. What we can do is put it in a context and consider additional ones. This will surely increase our objectivity and help us consider all the possibilities before making a decision. By doing this, we kill our darlings.

Our ego is the second obstacle to making good decisions. When we let our ego lead the decision-making process, we put our interests at the top. When the frame of the decision to be taken involves only ourselves, this can be okay. However, when we have to make a decision about something that will impact a country, an organization, a group of people, or even a family, we are biased if we do not neutralize our ego. Neutralizing our ego will prevent us from being judge and jury and so increase the legitimacy of our decisions.

Think critically and ask tons of questions. Ask questions to yourself and to others. Do it to eliminate vagueness and confusion and also to streamline your thinking. Ask questions to:

- enhance your knowledge
- enhance your comprehension of the situation
- analyze and evaluate the facts at your disposal
- synthesize the information available for use

Critical thinking as defined by the National Council for Excellence in Critical Thinking[22] is:

> ... the intellectually disciplined process of actively and skillfully conceptualizing, applying, analyzing, synthesizing, and/or evaluating information gathered from, or generated by, observation, experience, reflection, reasoning, or communication, as a guide to belief and action.

A shorter definition would be: Critical thinking is the objective analysis of facts to form a judgment.

Both definitions refer to the same process and skills.

As an example, critical thinking helps in defining if the cure is worse than the disease, considering the whole situation.[23]

Have the courage to ask the questions that may sound unethical, amoral, or outrageous. Asking a question with the right mindset—for example, to get a better view of the whole situation—cannot be outrageous, only the answer can be.

Considering all the skills needed to be a critical thinker, it would be tempting to consider that critical thinking is a hindrance to creativity. If we believe this, we imply that creative people are illogical and shallow. Taking the opposite view, creative people are vastly informed and often critical. You rarely get "thinking out of the box" by whirling aimlessly like the wind—it is usually after a session of critical thinking.

Think critically to find opportunities in a difficult situation. Make the best possible decisions and take informed actions.

Fourth job of the decision-maker: make the decision and set a feedback loop

It is possible to make a decision without having the full information. The only condition is to respect some principles: go step by step toward an ambitious goal, monitor the effects of the decision closely and regularly, and keep a plan B in mind before making the decision, in case the effects and impacts of the decision negatively diverge from your expectations.

To feel comfortable making a decision, it is essential to put in place a feedback loop that will allow you to characterize the outcomes (impacts, effects) of the decision and learn from them.

Here's the fundamental idea: great decisions don't always lead to great outcomes and bad decisions don't always lead to bad outcomes.

In the poker world, there is a tendency to equate the quality of a decision to the quality of its outcome. The two may not always be proportionately connected. A good decision can give a bad outcome and vice-versa.

Poker, unlike chess, is a game of incomplete information. In poker, you make decisions under conditions of uncertainty all the time. Valuable information remains hidden and one needs to develop the skill to make good decisions. There is also an element of luck involved in any outcome. Chess, on the other hand, contains no hidden information and involves very little luck.

Annie Duke, a former poker player, wrote about it in *Thinking in Bets*, an outstanding book on the decision-making process. "Life is poker, not chess," she wrote.[24] We live in a world that is closer

25

to poker than chess. When making a decision in the real world, uncertainty and luck play a role. The outcome is a combination of our skill to make quality decisions under uncertainty, and luck.

A great outcome does not make for a great decision. A great decision comes from a great process. A process where you attempt to represent your complete state of knowledge accurately.[25]

The way we should ideally think and form our beliefs is as follows:[26]

1. We hear something.
2. We think about it, examine it, determine whether it is true or false.
3. We form our beliefs.

But most of the time, it happens as follows:

1. We hear something.
2. We believe it is true.
3. Only sometimes, later, if we have the time or the inclination, we think about it, examine it, and determine whether it is true or false.
4. Instead of amending our beliefs to fit the new information, we do the opposite, altering our interpretation of that information to fit our beliefs.

We are human. And humans are "predictably irrational" as Dan Ariely mentions in his book.[27]

According to Annie Duke, a classical decision-making process is an open loop:

Belief ⟶ Bet ⟶ (Set of Outcomes)

Asking the question "Why did something happen the way it did?" and then trying to answer it is the best way to improve our mental models. Using the outcomes to refine our beliefs makes our decision-making process more accurate and robust.

However, outcomes tell us nothing about the quality of our decision. Unlike in chess, we cannot simply work backward from the quality of the outcome to determine the quality of our decisions. It can result from two things: the influence of skill and the influence of luck.

Incorporating the effect of skill, an updated version of the decision-making process will be a learning loop:

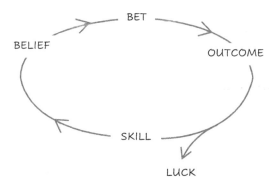

Figure 4: The quality of our decisions can result from the influence of skill and the influence of luck. Identify and remove the impact of luck from the learning process and consider only the elements that involve skills to form part of your learning loop.

Identify and remove the impact of luck from the learning process and consider only the elements that involve skills to form part of your learning loop.

Mental time travel

Business journalist and author Suzy Welch developed a popular tool known as "10–10–10" that has the effect of bringing the "future us" into our in-the-moment decisions.[28] When making a decision, start with the question: "What are the results of each of my options in 10 minutes? In 10 months? In 10 years?"

This tool reduces the weight of the emotion of the moment and brings more rationality to the decision-making process. Happenings of the recent past drive our emotional response much more than how we are doing overall. In psychology, it is called the "recency effect."

Hindsight bias

Let's say you have to make a decision that can result either in event A or event B. You make the decision BEFORE the outcome occurs; when either of the two events is probable. The problem is that we analyze the quality of the decision AFTER the outcome happened, based on the outcome, without considering the probability levels (information, knowledge, and beliefs) that were available when the decision was made. By doing this, we are determining the quality of a decision based on its outcome, which is potentially wrong. We have mixed up skill and luck. This creates an inaccurate learning loop, negatively affecting our future decision-making capabilities. This is a vicious circle.[29]

This is a common cognitive bias, known as the "hindsight bias," or the "I-knew-it-all-along" phenomenon, the tendency to perceive events as having been more predictable than they were.

You create a virtuous circle when you increase your awareness about the way you see the world (your stance, your worldview, your biases), the state of your knowledge (you don't have all the facts), and the fact that a decision is a bet and involves probabilities (the world is uncertain).

That's what it means to "think in bets" and what lies behind the meaning of "making smarter decisions."

Fifth job of the decision-maker: communicate and explain the decision transparently

When we make a decision on behalf of a community, the parties impacted by the decision not only need to hear it but also understand it.

"Understanding" differs from "agreeing." When making decisions, you cannot please everyone.

When people understand WHY (the hypothesis) and HOW (the reasoning) a decision has been taken, many non-constructive and unnecessary discussions may be avoided.

Sixth job of the decision-maker: Pilot the decision

Once you decide to jump from the top floor of a building, there are few possibilities to retrace your steps. However, this is not the case with all decisions. You can pilot most of them once you made them. The level of steering that is required is proportional to the entropy of the system.

A decision is not an end; it is a part of the initial conditions that will lead to the next one.

Part of the "fourth job" was to set a feedback loop to assess the evolution and validity of the hypothesis that led to the decision. Now is the time to activate that loop and understand if you need to re-assess the decision and "pivot" (change course), considering the additional information and insights. Closing the loop through this last job shows at least two benefits:

1. You keep control over the decision. You "pilot" the decision.
2. You learn and improve your model for the next time when you will have to make another decision.

Conclusion

Uncertainty is the only certainty there is. Deal with it and still make decisions. There is a process for it.

Follow this process to decide smartly. It will temporarily bring you out of your comfort zone, but in the long term, it will show significant benefits. For you, as an individual, and for the entire society that will benefit from you taking ownership and framing the future. Count less on others to tell you what you should do. Most of us would like others to decide for us and back us. But that's not the way it works.

And for those spectators who are just watching others take the lead and make decisions, sometimes even criticizing the decisions and the people who made them, ask yourself a simple question:

How can I become the one "in the arena"?[30]

This question is referring to a speech Theodore Roosevelt delivered at the Sorbonne in Paris in April 1910, from which here is a brief excerpt:

It is not the critic who counts; not the man who points out how the strong man stumbles, or where the doer of deeds could have done them better. The credit belongs to the man who is actually in the arena, whose face is marred by dust and sweat and blood; who strives valiantly; who errs, who comes short again and again, because there is no effort without error and shortcoming; but who does actually strive to do the deeds; who knows great enthusiasms, the great devotions; who spends himself in a worthy cause; who at the best knows in the end the triumph of high achievement, and who at the worst, if he fails, at least fails while daring greatly, so that his place shall never be with those cold and timid souls who neither know victory nor defeat.[31]

Go into the arena and make good decisions. That's the best way for you to contribute.

(Jean-Marie Buchilly)

4
GIVING LEGS TO YOUR IDEAS

There's always an animating idea behind an organization. Think of Apple. It showcases the idea that technology should be easy to use. Aspiring entrepreneurs often brim with passion, driven by the power of such ideas and their competence in that particular domain. They storm the hill in search of funds, teams, and tools that'll give their ideas legs. After a certain point in time, they stumble on their journey without knowing where they're heading. They find themselves drowning in actions and lose sight of the forest, for the trees. They get sucked in the micro measurement of their actions, feeling quite lost.

Putting the cart before the horse

What they don't realize is that they put the cart before the horse. They put execution before strategy, often even mistaking execution for strategy.

What prompted Henry Ford to famously tell his Model-T customers that they could have any color as long as it was black? Why did Dolby Laboratories decide to license its proprietary technology to product developers like Sony or Bose instead of launching their own products? What drove Ryanair to choose secondary airports or remove free meals or minimize legroom from its offer?

These are critical decisions entwined in strategy that defines organizations. Strategy is the map that helps organizations to position themselves on key factors that help to out-compete other firms that operate in the same domain, sell similar products or services, and attract the same customers. It helps them to strip away non-essential actions (like Ford's "black color only" position) and focus on those essential elements that give companies their competitive advantage.

If the executive team does not think at the organizational level from the start but instead rushes to execution, they might find themselves lost in course of time and feel directionless. The strategy design process is like devising a compass for the organization, but it can't be set in stone. Startups possess the valuable gift of agility when compared to the incumbents and should exercise this gift well in the case of strategy too. Since they maneuver in uncertain terrain with very limited resources, they might want to revisit their compass once in a while to make sense of their positioning.

The IKEA case

In the late 1940s, Ingvar Kamprad started a mail-order business in Sweden that was built on the philosophy that one can build a profitable business even by selling at a low price. This understanding came to him much earlier in life, when he was just seven. He would get his aunt to get him matches in bulk from Stockholm and he would sell them in his village neighborhood, making a profit.[32]

He picked the furniture business and found an opportunity in attracting those customers who would not buy expensive furniture in the then-existing high-price market. In choosing such customers, Kamprad cast his net in the blue ocean where his competitors did not venture. Though he faced backlash from them initially, he held on to his mission of "low-price, good quality" furniture.

IKEA did many things to keep their costs low. They shifted to Poland for supply and manufacturing that reduced their costs considerably; they chose to locate themselves out of town as the land was cheaper; they used the flat-pack idea (borrowed it from another innovator), and even created complex organizational structures to manage tax. Since they were so clear on what they wanted to be, they could set out to maximize ways of achieving their aim. And IKEA was successful.

But when IKEA decided to venture into countries like India and China, many things changed for them. For example, the meaning of affordability or thin wallet for IKEA and these countries were very different. Their cultures were distinct too. IKEA could not approach these countries with the same strategy they had for countries like the United States. The tastes of these markets, the materials suitable for these geographies, and the affordability factor called for a new strategy. Some fundamental parts of IKEA's old strategy had to be changed. They could not sail through these rough seas holding on to the old plank.

Ideas don't have "legs"

Imagine making a flip book. Essentially, you drew the same character but changed their position bit by bit on every new page. The images you drew did not animate by themselves; the animation effect came

34

about only when you flipped the book. This is what happens to great ideas and strategies. Unless they are executed well, they continue to remain motionless on paper (and in our minds, too). For your idea to spring to life, to grow their legs, to move, and to move fast, you first need your execution plan in place.

In Graham Kenny's *Harvard Business Review* article, "5 Simple Rules for Strategy Execution," he enlists the following rules that one can use to ensure proper execution. Your execution plan should be as follows:

1. Keep your focus narrow as wanting to do too many things may set you up for failure.

2. Delineate actions in your action plan—"staff engagement" is an ongoing ac tivity, whereas "staff engagement during New Year's Eve" can be measured by an end date.

3. Build ownership—ownership drives accountability.

4. Consciously discern strategy meetings from execution meetings—daily grind takes precedence otherwise.

5. Monitor and measure.

Strategy and execution are two sides of a coin. The former is planned at the organizational level and needs hungry, fearless individuals who are passionately focused on growth to execute it successfully. But let's not forget that strategy is relative and ephemeral and successful implementation will evoke responses from the competition. So, you cannot sleep over your strategy thinking you found the ideal and long-lasting one. It's imperative to keep exploring the blue ocean.[33]

(Meenakshi Babu)

5
UNDERSTAND YOUR CUSTOMER:
STATUS, WORLDVIEWS, BELIEFS

Customers are the most important stakeholder in any business. A business functions and sustains itself only because it has paying customers who benefit from it. Self-made millionaire and author Harvey Mackay says, "No business can stay in business without customers."[34] Many innovators and founders lose sight of this at the beginning and put the bulk of their thinking into their idea. Their passion for their idea leads them straight into building a product or a service around it. They either develop and launch their product without customer validation, or busy themselves with creating business plans and pitch decks to seek investments for building their product. Their attention is more focused on securing funding and as a result, they create a great business plan and pitch deck, geared toward highlighting the market size, market penetration, and their ability to execute the business plan. With so much already on their plate, they simply don't have enough time to go deeper into who their future customers will be, what their pain points are, and how the product/service they are developing can ease those pain points and create real value to that community of people who would ultimately pay for all the fuel that goes into running their business. Many times, they end up developing a superb product or service that lacks a market need—one that no one is willing to pay for. This "idea to product" centric approach is one of the principal reasons many startups fail.

That you may create more certainty in your idea, there is a subtle but powerful approach to take. It involves upfront work and a scientific outlook that most entrepreneurs tend to ignore. What, if you put your customer in the center of your idea from the very beginning, and work on every detail of your idea development toward launching *with* your customer?

Make your key idea an entry point to your customer-discovery process. To lead you to the real pain points your customers have in your idea's domain. The best ideas are the ones that solve the paying customers' biggest problems in each domain. If the entrepreneur finds the *big problems of customers* rather than *a problem*, then they have put the customer at the heart of the process. Do this *before* looking for a product/service solution and *before* building a prototype or an MVP.[35]

Your business is not about you, it is about your customers—and the added value and benefits embedded in your assertion. Through your business, you are creating a promise about the fact that you care, and sharing a worldview and a core belief with your audience.

But who is this audience you are targeting? You are not building your product for everybody. There is no mass market. The essential question to ask yourself at the very beginning is: "Who is it for?"

Put a lot of attention on the status, worldviews, and beliefs of the community you are trying to serve.

Status is our narrative, the story we tell ourselves about ourselves, and about the world. Our status strongly depends on our worldview and beliefs. Worldview is the way of seeing the world—your point of view. It is not objective, supported by facts. Worldviews are subjective, value-based reflections and comprise how you perceive the world around you, based on your unique experiences and beliefs.

If you believe what they believe and if you know what they know, you will do what they do. This is a statement of empathy. And "innovation is a by-product of empathy," as Bernadette Jiwa states in her book *Meaningful: The Story of Ideas That Fly*.[36]

Put yourself in the shoes of the people and communities you are trying to serve and seek to see the world as they do. You will not be playing in the rational world selling feature "A" for a certain amount of money. No, you will sell feelings, status, and connections.

> People don't believe what you tell them.
> They rarely believe what you show them.
> They often believe what their friends tell them.
> They always believe what they tell themselves.
>
> – Seth Godin[37]

That you may bring your change to the world, you need to make some assumptions about what your customers believe, and what their narrative and worldviews look like. You can't hear the noise in their heads, but you can watch what they do and make some guesses.

The way you see the world isn't nearly as important as the worldview of those you seek to serve. The way their mind works differs from yours, and their worldview is always stronger than the story you will tell them.

People either protect or challenge the status quo. Before making change happen, you need to understand the stories people are telling themselves.

(*Jean-Marie Buchilly*)

6
WHY WAIT? GO
FUND YOURSELF

When Shyjal Raazi, the founder of Collect.chat, quit his stable, high-paying job at a startup in Dubai, he already had the idea of his business shaped up and validated with customers. Collect.chat is a human-friendly, interactive chatbot solution for businesses to engage website visitors in conversations rather than filling boring forms, to collect leads. In the early days, they were 100 percent bootstrapped,[38] and continue to remain so.

The journey to making his product didn't happen all of a sudden. It happened while working with a friend in the travel industry as a side hustle. His friend Saran approached him one day, saying, "I am getting good traffic on my website, but none of those are converting to customers. Can you help?" Shyjal has a software background, and this was a problem from his area of interest and expertise. He did a bit of research on the solutions out there within the conversational revolution and chatbots. They did a quick trial with a chatbot widget, added it to the website's landing page, and within a few weeks, observed a spike in the conversion rates. Shyjal had found a problem worth solving, and a solution that seemed to solve the problem well.

Shyjal had earlier worked as a software developer with quite a few companies, but always had this lingering feeling that was not what he wanted to do with his life. Today, most people work in the technology industry just as they would do in any other industry. They follow a 40-hour workweek, write codes to build things within their narrow domain, earn their salary, and go about their life. Shyjal believes that a software developer can do much more than this. Anyone with the right inclination can build and run an entire company, and not just operate as a typical "engineer" in a day job. Engineers are the actual makers of the product and should act like one. All you need to run the show is a laptop and a good internet connection. There is a paradigm shift in the way software is built nowadays, and indie makers are empowered with all the tools they need. The only variable being the intent on the part of the maker. Shyjal wanted to taste the freedom that every creator deserves and do something where he could feel the impact of his work and take control of his time. So, this adventure started as a journey to seek freedom.

He continued to build parts of Collect.chat while holding his job. He did his research on the existing market and realized that if he could come up with something solid, he could build a company of his own. He focused on getting to a shippable product, rather than making it perfect. After weeks of coding sprints, he had his first MVP. He likes to call it an MLP—Minimum Lovable Product. Something that people loved, and not something that would be abandoned after a user tried it once.

Luckily for him, at the same time as he started working on the project, his college buddy Aslam had quit his corporate job with plans for higher studies. Aslam's skills perfectly complemented Shyjal's, and having earlier worked on several minor projects together, Shyjal knew that their values and aptitude matched well. Shyjal invited him to become a co-founder and with Aslam on board, things got much smoother.

At that point, it was vital for them to validate the product, get to product–market fit at the earliest. They had to see if his product worked the same way it did for Saran's website.

He launched the MLP to the market using platforms like ProductHunt. The day it launched on ProductHunt, it ended up being the #4 product of the day. Over 250 websites started using the bot on day one, and it started growing virally. Shyjal thought of adding a payment code as well but decided that this did not directly contribute to the MLP. Instead, he created a dummy pricing page telling interested customers that the first three months were free. People signed up for premium plans without actually paying. This was an enormous leap for his product validation. He was building a user base valuable in further optimizing his MLP. He waited for the initial reactions and feedback and worked to improve the product using this feedback loop.

Once he was fully prepared to board this emotional rollercoaster, he registered his company officially and quit his job. This was not the first time he had quit a stable job to go after his dreams. But this time, he was more confident, knowing that he had something that people wanted and it added value to the world.

Since he came from a software background and had toyed around with other project ideas in the past, it was easier for Shyjal to come up with the MLP in the way he wanted to. Not every entrepreneur has that background. If you are in a stage where you have figured out a problem to solve, then the biggest investment you need to put in is "time." Building an MVP in the software industry is not very tough. You can hire talent to build the MVP from anywhere in the world. What matters is execution. The moment you solve one problem, other problems will pile up. A true entrepreneur should never lose sight of the original problem and focus all their efforts to solve the *actual* problem.

Shyjal started a venture of his own to gain freedom. Financial freedom, freedom of choice, personal freedom, freedom to work from anywhere in the world, and more. He knew that staying bootstrapped would be critical to getting this freedom.

Not all business ideas are created equal. While some ideas need a heavy cash flow to lift off the ground, let alone fly, many (in today's SaaS[39]-based world, perhaps most) businesses can begin their first flights with relatively little cash. The cash you may either already have tucked away somewhere in your savings or may be able to get from family and friends. If there is an option to bootstrap your business, then take that option. Bootstrap to sustain your business through customer revenues. If the market you are looking into is large enough, you can always get a chunk of it and never bother about external debts and investments. It will give you the peace of mind and freedom that usually gets lost when you're answerable to your investors.

Most times, if you want to dominate the market or penetrate a market that is already dominated, then you have to burn cash; to run ads and reach the audience. For such ventures, the only way forward is to take external funding. External funding (venture capital or otherwise) might be also required at a stage where you are looking for high or exponential growth. For instance, sometimes you must act quickly to get attention. When COVID-19 struck the world, many companies acted quickly to gain traction. To capitalize on such scenarios, you need funds in hand. So even though you can stay bootstrapped in the early stages, you may need funding in the later stages to achieve this high growth.

The best approach is to delay investments or funding as much as possible. There is no need to take a strict NO or YES policy. First, we need the business to find its roots and get some grip. Then for growth, we can think about raising some capital. It's up to you to make this decision.

When one looks at the startup world, one observes a common theme in the life of VC-funded startups:

- You are always answerable to the investors.
- You focus on making the best pitches for your startup but forget to make your product or service as good as possible.
- You burn money faster than it comes in and once the source dries out, you scramble around looking for other sources of investment.

In a nutshell, if you are a founder of a funded startup, you are always on the run and can never settle until you become cash positive. Some don't stop even then.

This situation might sound like an exaggeration, but it is close to the truth. Every week or so, Shyjal gets an email from an investment firm asking if he's looking for investment. He turns them down. His aim, his WHY, is to make a product that people can use with minimal effort and something that they and their end customers will love. The fewer the number of people involved in the decision-making process, the more focused he and his team can be. That's how they have managed their product and customers for the last three years. Bootstrapping has helped him stay focused on his original goal. And yes, they are still bootstrapped and hope to do so for the foreseeable future.

Today they are operating on a subscription model and their business is thriving. Since they put all their effort into building a product that their customer would love, they were not much into marketing. People came in, used their product, and paid, without a sales team, with no push. Since their product was so useful to the customer, the customers made sure to spread the word of their existence and bring other users to the website. Once enough revenue started coming in, they reinvested heavily to further improve their product.

By keeping their customers at the center of everything they did, Shyjal and his team got three things in return:

- customer retention
- customer referral
- upsells

Bootstrapping helped them keep their costs to a bare minimum. When you don't have a lot, you cannot afford to waste. Austerity brings discipline. This helps in focusing on things that matter. You are accountable only to your customer, and no one else. Bootstrapping is like growing organically—you let the fruit grow naturally at its own pace. VC-funding is akin to injecting supplements to grow and ripen the fruit faster.

Starting up can be hard, especially when you don't have investor money to run. But the feeling of freedom, excitement, and ownership is incomparable.

(*Shyjal Raazi*)

7
DO YOU NEED A CO-FOUNDER?

Solo founders are inspiring—Pieter Levels at Nomad List, Josh Pigford at Baremetrics, even Jeff Bezos at Amazon. But startup life is hard. If things go south, it can be an emotional rollercoaster. Staying motivated when you are a solo founder can be tough.

If you are someone who believes it's better to do it all on your own, think through it one more time. You're probably more skilled in a few areas whereas, in others, other people can do parts of the work; if not better, perhaps at least someone well educated in the area will do it quicker than you. This will give you more time to free up your mind and work on things that only you can do. Building a startup means you have to know a little about everything, but it does not mean the way to go is to do everything on your own. Think through when making your arrangements. Focus on doing what you do the best, which also is what brings you the most joy. Are you great with numbers? Do taxes and VAT make you want to dance? Are you down to learn to code or build a website with YouTube as your mentor? If not, consider choosing a partner interested in those things. And if your plan is to go solo in business, maybe it's better to pay someone else to do the initial setup, and then show you the everyday how-to. Spread your focus and energy wisely.

Some entrepreneurs find it better to have a co-founder. If you are one who thinks a co-founder may add value to your company, read on.

The search for the perfect co-founder or partner can take various solution paths. Each founder finds their co-founder in a unique, seemingly coincidental way. It follows the synchronization between the qualitative and quantitative side of the founder or partner.

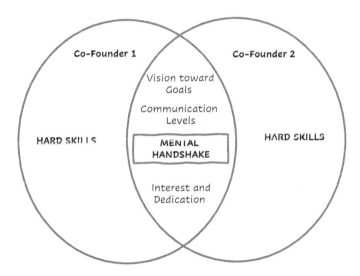

Figure 5: How do you find the right co-founder? In addition to hard skills, a "mental handshake"—the vision, emotion, passion, and zeal of the cofounders toward the startup—play an equivalent role. A strong synchronization between the two is crucial for success.

Many founders argue that skills (quantitative side) of the co-founder or partner is of utmost importance as it sets the pillars for the startup's growth. But in most successful startups it is the qualitative side or the "mental handshake" (the emotion, passion, and zeal of the co-founders toward the startup) playing an equivalent role. The stronger the synchronization between the two sides (qualitative and quantitative) the higher is the probability of success with the startup. Making a list in terms of hard skills and soft skills counters one side of the coin, or in other terms "the quantitative side."

This drives us to some direct areas where these ingredients can be easily discovered:

- **First-level connections**: School friends, college friends, and previous or present company employees. Close, trusted individuals. If you are looking for a co-founder, if possible, start with someone from college, someone you already know or have worked with earlier who you can trust. This way, even if you have disagreements or debates, you can continue to be friends.

- **Second-level connections**: The references or contacts of your close contacts or the references of first-level connections. We can trust their references.

- **Third-level connections**: If the above two steps are failed tries then comes the path of interacting with specific stakeholders directly concerned with the startup idea. Examples include discussions with mentors, meeting industry experts, and incubators. Their guidance or references increase the success ratio of the venture as they are well aware of the situation and the quantitative and qualitative side required for the startup.

Offering value exchange is an important aspect in finding a co-founder or partner. The answer goes hand-in-hand with the mental handshake. The co-founder must understand the project and its implications, and the end goal of the startup. The mental handshake is the key. Supporting this is the factor of equity distribution (after a certain level of success of the startup).

Take care when selecting your co-founder. Indeed, one of the major reasons for startups to fail is the falling out of co-founders. As with many things in life, differences arise over money and fairness. If it looks like the startup will make money, then the greed in human nature can kick in.

In the beginning, when it's all new and everything is rosy, founders are quite arbitrary with equity stakes and seek what they think is a fair stake that will keep their co-founder motivated. Usually, the founder has had the original idea and takes the majority stake. This gets set in stone forever, at least until investors get involved. Like many relationships in life, it's a happy beginning but, as time passes and challenges arise, situations can get tense. If the co-founder is perceived to be not pulling their weight, or if the co-founder feels they are hard done by, then tensions can surface and the fairness around the original equity stake can be a major bone of contention that can lead to co-founders leaving, losing motivation and the very existence of the startup may be at risk. Many startups fail this way.

Is there a way to overcome this kind of situation? The dynamic equity model is one solution worth considering. It is based on acknowledging and accordingly changing the equity distribution as founder contributions change and accumulate. An example of this is the Slicing Pie model by Mike Moyer.[40]

Slicing Pie Model

In this model, inputs of time, money, equipment, and intellectual property are valued at market rates to produce a total size of the input equity of a company, with each co-founder having a dynamic share or slice of the input equity. The model is based on the premise that if the startup was fully funded, what would it pay each person to do the job with the hours, intellectual property, and equipment they put in. It helps you calculate the value of your founder equity share and allocate equity to all your co-founders, employees, and partners. The main exception here is when someone puts real money into the startup. In that case, it is valued as high-risk capital and its value is more than the time it would take to earn that money. These models also consider situations such as co-founders leaving the company, being pushed out, bad behavior.

Whichever model you choose, it ultimately revolves around human nature and situations vary from case to case. If you can be the dominant equity holder in the traditional model, then it probably pays to push for this as long as you can keep your co-founder(s) happy and motivated. The dynamic model, where ongoing commitment and value are rewarded, is a fairer arrangement but may not suit you, the founder, if you think you would benefit more from the traditional model.

Whichever model you decide upon, once outside funding is obtained, your equity model will need to be negotiated and implemented per the dynamics of the investment ecosystem.

(*Aditya Bhatnagar, Simon Krystman, Susanna Schumacher,* and *Shyjal Raazi*)

III

STEP INTO THE ARENA

8
THE INNOVATOR'S MODEL

Once you have built a clear picture of who your customer is and laid the groundwork, start developing your idea by placing your customer at the center. From the very beginning, have every detail of development geared toward launching and growing with your customers in mind.

Innovator's Model

This book introduces a powerful philosophy for continuous optimization of your business that starts from your first idea and applies as you scale-up and grow. We call it the "Innovator's Model." You may use it as your guiding mantra throughout your business development journey. It gives you a common cyclic framework for the three stages of innovation development: idea development, product development, and scale-up. The loops are inspired by Susanna Nissar's visualization of the design thinking loop,[41] Simon Krystman's Customer Launch Philosophy (a concept introduced for the first time through this book), and Eric Ries' Lean Startup[42] methodology.

The Innovator's Model places the customer at the center,

and each optimization phase is rooted in empathizing with the customer. No matter where you are on your business journey, use this model to empathize with your customers, validate your product with them, and optimize it.

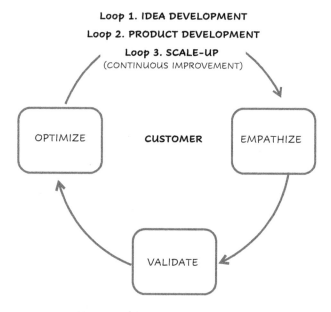

Figure 6: Innovator's Model is customer-centric. It consists of three loops representing the three stages of development, from idea to product to scale-up. Each optimization phase is rooted in first empathizing with the customer to thoroughly understand their circumstances, status, beliefs, and worldviews, validating it with the customer, and optimizing it to maximize the value and engagement of your customer with your product.

Through this model, you are integrating research into every phase of your business journey. By using this approach, your solution will align with your customers' needs, and with your organization's purpose and your WHY.

You will go through several iterations of these loops. In each iteration, you switch between understanding the problem and exploring the solution, which allows you to determine the root cause of the problem you are solving. The quality of your outcome will be in direct proportion to your ability to identify the right problem to solve.

Stage Zero: Understand your customer and empathize

The model begins with Stage Zero where you define the target customer groups and the domain for the idea. For example, if the idea is to sell a new non-alcoholic tequila, the domain can be beverages, lifestyle, or health. As discussed in the previous chapters pay complete attention to understanding who your customer is and what their needs are within the domain of your idea. Are they Zoomers (or Generation Z)? Are they pubs and restaurants? If Zoomers, what are their specific characteristics? What do you think they identify themselves with? What are their worldviews and beliefs? Spend time thinking this through, thoroughly. Identify people who you think will fit into your idea of your ideal customer. Meet them, speak with them (don't tell them anything about your business or idea at this point). Give yourself a week to only think about them and observe your thoughts. Put yourself in their shoes. Go out and experience what your customer is experiencing. Empathize with them. When you empathize with your customer, understand their circumstances and worldviews, you go beyond looking at them as a set of people with general demographic similarities; you find ways to build genuinely meaningful bonds with them. To design and create meaningful products for them. The foundation of this model is to understand the traits, driving forces, and pain points of your customer.

Consider Stage Zero as a constantly active stage throughout

your journey. You NEED to continuously and ceaselessly empathize with your customers. Always keep their needs in mind, no matter which stage you are in.

First Loop: Customer Launch Philosophy for Idea Development

Simon Krystman, a serial entrepreneur and startup mentor, through his years of experience founding and mentoring startups, observes one common loophole in the strategy and approach of most startups that often lead them to failure. They follow an idea–product-centric approach, developing the product with investors in mind.

With the Customer Launch Philosophy, you put your customer at the center of your idea development process. We call this customer-centric innovation. This comes before moving to the prototype/MVP/product phase. It is in line with design thinking and complements "Lean Thinking" when you develop your product.

Stage One: Validate your key observation with your customers

The first stage is to frame your idea to your customer groups for feedback, focusing to find out if it is something they want, can't get elsewhere, or would prefer a variation. You investigate whether this is the most pressing pain point or need for the customer group in your idea domain. You present your idea to your customer.

If this is a big need or pain point to be solved, then it is important to investigate the price points at this stage. If it takes a lot of money to produce something that the customer groups are only willing to pay a little for, it will all come down to nothing.

This is the "hypothesis testing" stage. You are testing the validity of your proposition directly with your customer. There is a possibility that your customers may give you a more pressing pain point or a need to solve, or a better idea than your original idea.

Market research such as surveys and big data analysis are useful tools. But for understanding the value of something that doesn't yet exist in the market, you need to do qualitative research. Qualitative research methods like semi-structured interviews, observations, or co-creation with potential customers let you gain an in-depth understanding of the gap and the opportunity. While quantitative methods help you with big trends, the WHAT, qualitative methods help you with the WHY and HOW. When you are doing qualitative research, remember to ask open-ended questions with lots of "why, where, how, when ..." to collect your insights. Listen and let the potential customer lead the conversation. Your role is to be the facilitator, suggesting discussion areas and steer the conversation toward the gap and opportunity connected to your idea. When you hear that similar things seem important to several people, your insights start to saturate—a pattern of the same needs, expectations, or behavior start to emerge.

A useful tool this early in the idea development process, and a great complement to semi-structured interviews, is trigger material. Trigger materials are illustrations or other artifacts that trigger a response from the user. By adding visuals to the discussion, you are helping the potential customer to put words on their abstract thoughts. Trigger material is not to be mixed up with prototyping or testing, though. The aim with the trigger material is not to get yes or no answers to a prototype, but rather to understand what is relevant to the potential customers. Qualitative research methods can be tricky to learn, but if you are willing to, you will learn with some practice. They will be some of the most useful techniques during your entire business journey, as they help you empathize with your customers and understand your solution from their point of view.

Take this process to the next level by using one of the many tried and tested idea validation techniques. These techniques range in cost, effort, run time, and validation strength. They are "action validation" techniques that need a user to act—submit their email address for more information, select a pre-order button, and so on—and not just fill out a survey form. This is what makes these techniques powerful and effective.

One of the most well-known case studies of action validation is the video explainer used by Dropbox.[43] The people at Dropbox weren't completely sure they could develop the technology at the time and wanted to assess customer need before spending lots of money on R&D. They validated their idea by producing an explainer video and putting it on a landing page. The video explained their proposed product, stitched together with mock-ups to give the viewer an idea of what the product would do and look like. It drove hundreds of thousands of people to the website. The beta waiting list went up from 5,000 to 75,000 people overnight. By signing up, customers overwhelmingly validated the idea, and the Dropbox team then spent time and money engineering the product with confidence that customers would want it.

A basic form of action validation is a "Coming Soon" landing page that clearly states the value proposition, benefits, and a call to action by asking for an email address to be supplied for more information. This is low-level validation, but by requiring the user to do something rather than just move on, you get an idea about the level of interest. You can create several variations of this such as a "Pricing" page preceding the "Coming Soon" page, adding steps to the registration flow to test motivation levels and to find out more.

In the "Broken Promise" variation, you inform your new subscribers that they are part of an exclusive group and explicitly ask them not to share the idea with others. By comparing the list of people contacted with the list of sign-ups, you can measure the virality of your idea. When people come across an idea or a product they love, they can't help themselves and will automatically share it with others, despite you telling them not to.

Variations of action validation technique include waiting lists, pre-order forms (mock sale), pocket prototypes.

As a way of validating if people (the crowd) want your idea before you make it, crowdfunding is another powerful technique. You are collecting actual money, usually put in escrow, to create your idea, validating a customer's need. Kickstarter is an example of this type of idea validation. A variation of crowdfunding that may be even more powerful for collecting data on idea-customer fit is the pre-sale of products (the equivalent of purchase orders) from a website. You offer your idea or concept in the same way as if it existed but in a limited edition. If enough people purchase your product, it validates your customer's need, and you can then create the product and have it delivered. CrowdMall is an example of this technique.

You can collect and analyze useful metrics such as customer profile data, conversion rates, bounce rates, session time, conversions based on traffic source.

Stage Two: *Optimize your key idea with your customers*

After you have had the discussions with your customers, and after you have run your idea validation campaign (if you run one), you need to transform your notes into insights and use them as a launchpad for optimizing your first idea of what your service or product should look like in its first version.

Here is a simple way of doing this:

- Headline and group the key findings (physically with post-its or digitally) to explore themes and patterns.

- Explore each theme and rephrase it as a brief statement. The statement can look something like this: "[CUSTOMER] needs to [NEED] because [INSIGHT]." This represents the GAP.

- Formulate a "How might we?" question from these statements. This question will serve as a launchpad for your idea optimization. Simply put, a "How might we?" in front of the statement—"How might we help [CUSTOMER] to [NEED]?"

- Use your original idea as the answer to the "How might we?" question and explore if there is a scope to tweak your idea to make it better at solving the need.

Before you start with idea optimization, embrace a mindset of curiosity and save your judgments for later. Don't be too rigid about your original idea—be open to ideate further. You may realize that there is a far better way of solving the problem, and your idea is not the right one. Your customer may give you an idea better than your original one—be open to the possibilities.

Select a couple of the new variations/ideas and move back to Stage One. Validate them with your customers. Eventually moving from Stage One to Stage Two and back to Stage One will refine your idea for the customers' needs and pain points, providing you with a customer-validated idea as the foundation of your Customer Launch.

If you do not have an original idea to start with, this method will still be helpful to you. Choose a domain you are passionate about or knowledgeable in. Begin your journey by defining your customer group in Stage Zero. Go to Stage One to investigate their most pressing pain points. Use this as the starting point to ideate the best ways of addressing the pain points. Include any ideas your customer may have given you. Refine them by iterating between Stages One and Two.

This method is only a small part of the prelaunch stage of a founder's journey. You can complete it quickly—within a couple of weeks—if properly designed and executed. There will hardly be any upfront investment, other than your time. But it will give you a definite idea about your customers' needs and improve your chances of arriving at a solution that best addresses those needs. A lot more will remain to be done—prototypes/MVPs/products to be developed, competition and market analysis to be undertaken, robust financials to ensure feasibility, business plans to be created. A team will have to be assembled. However, unlike most startups, the customer will be at the center of the idea and your intellectual property.

Most startups fail eventually. Most startups don't begin with putting the customer at the center, they begin with putting the product at the center.

Second Loop: Lean Product Development

In line with design thinking, and with an approach similar to the first loop, the second loop is based on a user-centered development process and contains elements of empathizing with the users, experimenting with your MVP, and working in iterations where learning compounds over time.

Jump onto the second loop once you have arrived at the right idea addressing the right pain points. This is where you begin spending time and resources to create a first tangible version of your product—your MVP.

The second loop starts with your idea. This may or may not be your original idea, but the one you have arrived at after iterating within the first loop. Because your idea has now been validated by your customers, you are confident about what you are going to make and have a clear picture of what will constitute the core benefits of your product. With that picture in mind, create your MVP.

When you start your MVP testing process with a customer-validated idea, the number of iterations in creating, validating, and optimizing your MVP will be much less. This means you will significantly save time and resources when iterating your MVP. This makes the Innovator's Model so much more powerful and practical. You know what you are going to make, well before you make it. You have a ready-made road map of what to build. You will be launching your product with your customer.

Stage Three: Create your key object

Your focus at this stage is to have an MVP that you can use to evaluate the impact of your product on your customer. The principal object of this phase is to fail fast, if at all, and at a low cost. Your MVP does not need to be advanced or take a long time to create. What is more important is to create something that you can bring to your customer, get their reactions, go back and adjust. The simpler and sketchier it is, the more open will it be for the users to co-create and imagine their own version of it. Also, the simpler the MVP is, the more open you will be to changing your ideas. This is your key object. Unlike a prototype or a concept test, you are creating your MVP not just to answer design and technical feasibility questions, but to test and validate your fundamental business hypotheses, not within your internal team, but with your customers. It may be difficult for you as an entrepreneur to place something so raw in front of your customers. You may have wanted to introduce a high-quality mainstream product to your customers, not a ragtag that is used only by a tiny niche of people willing to try much before it is ready. But how do you know which attributes of your product will be perceived as worthwhile by your customer? What constitutes a "high-quality mainstream product"?

With an MVP you are not placing your best foot forward. You are instead exhibiting an unfinished, imperfect product. The fundamental idea behind your MVP is that any additional work beyond what you need to learn about the value of your product is a waste, no matter how important you or your team think of it to be. Your goal is to minimize the total time through the second loop. Avoid the temptation to overbuild. Instead, simplify your MVP.

Stage Four: Validate your key object with your customers

Place your MVP, a real, tangible product, in front of your customer.

This is a repetition of the process you followed in Stage One, except that now you are presenting an actual product. Remember, your MVP is your first product. You are now in the market, selling your product. This may be a bare minimum of a product, far from perfect, probably full of bugs, but nevertheless, it is. This is what you are placing in front of your customer and asking them to use. Your goal is to see how your customer behaves with your product, and through a scientific and objective approach, validate and optimize your product. The focus here is not to sell your product to as many customers as possible, but to test if they perceive your product as valuable, and how to maximize that value and engagement of your customer with your product.

Back in my Ph.D. days, we routinely ran optimization experiments to arrive at the best conditions for the desired outcome. We would start by first defining a hypothesis about the effect of a factor on an outcome and test it to decide whether to accept or reject the hypothesis. If the results indicated we accept the hypothesis, we would then optimize the conditions for the most desirable outcome. My research work focused on breaking down biomass (e.g., plant waste) and using the released components to produce value-added chemicals. Let's say I start with a hypothesis that if I heat the biomass for a sufficiently long time, its structure will break. You see, biomass has a tough structure and unless in the stomach of a cow or a horse, it doesn't break that easily. So, I define time and temperature as the factors that likely will affect biomass breakdown. I heat the biomass at various temperatures and for various amounts of time, and at the end of each experiment, I measure the extent of biomass breakdown. I use untreated biomass as the baseline or the control.

Analyzing all this data tells me if the treatment has any effect on the biomass. It may happen that no matter how long and how much I heat the biomass, nothing happens. Its structure remains the same as the untreated biomass. In that case, I will need to reject my hypothesis. I conclude that time and temperature, within the range tested, do not have a significant effect on biomass. If I still believe that time and temperature should have an impact, I will design a second set of experiments, for a different set of time and temperature, and repeat. If in this time I see a change in biomass structure, then my hypothesis is validated, within the range tested. I can then work on optimizing the process for time and temperature that will yield maximum breakdown of biomass.

Consider your work with your MVP as a set of scientific experiments. For each experiment, you identify the key factor(s) that may affect customer behavior vis-à-vis your product, and frame hypotheses. At this MVP stage, the factors you are experimenting with are not features of your product—an MVP by definition does not have many features. It is the core benefit your MVP is offering to the customer. The parts on which everything depends. As Eric Ries explains in his book *The Lean Startup*, these will be your "value hypothesis" and your "growth hypothesis." At this stage, you are ensuring that you are building something that your customer will want (your product delivers value to your customers once they use it—the value hypothesis) and understanding how new customers will discover your product (how it will spread among your customers, from early adopters to mass adoption—the growth hypothesis).

Choosing the right metrics

To test any hypothesis, you must have the right metrics to measure the right outcome. To measure the extent of biomass breakdown, I measured the change in the composition of biomass. There are multiple components in biomass; I would measure all of them and compare their amounts to the untreated sample.

Be very careful when choosing your metrics. How do you know if your product is of value to your customer? The most obvious way might be to track the number of new customers you are adding every week or month. You may see a marginal increase in the number of new customers added every day and a corresponding increase in total revenue. You are thrilled. You jump to think that your product is on its path to becoming a market success. But does an increase in the number of new customers mean your product is perceived as valuable? You may have used certain marketing and advertising tools, or an expensive public relations push, to attract these new customers. The increase in the number of new customers does not by itself indicate the value of your product to them. There are no direct cause-and-effect inferences to be drawn here.

The questions you should be asking, which also are your core hypotheses are:

1. Does my product matter to my customers? (Your *value* hypothesis.)
2. Can I build a sustainable business with it? (Your *growth* hypothesis.)

The answer to these questions lies not in the gross metrics, but in other details. How many customers were interested in your product and got registered? How many of them went on to take the indicated action? How engaged were they with your product? How much time did they spend on the product? What were the retention rates? What were the churn rates (fraction of customers who failed to remain engaged with your product)? What were the referral rates? A monetary exchange may not be the only indicator of value.

For companies like Facebook and LinkedIn, customers' time and attention indicate the value of the product. The raw amount of time Facebook's active users spend on the site, and the sheer number of users who come back every day validate its value hypothesis—that customers find Facebook valuable. In its early days, the rate at which Facebook spread across universities in a very small amount of time validated its growth hypothesis. Facebook at the time didn't have a business model, it wasn't generating any revenue. But investors funded it, nonetheless, because it was acquiring new customers every day while paying nothing in customer acquisition—and because the existing customers were exhibiting high engagement. It was a valuable proposition.

When you work on hypotheses and validate them with the help of customer data, you empirically demonstrate whether your assumptions hold or not. Startups thrive in uncertainty; by following this customer data-driven approach, you are attempting to tame the uncertainty to some extent, a rationale to work upon, a path to take.

As with the biomass experiment earlier, there is always a possibility that your hypotheses will stand refuted. It may so happen that despite all your attempts, you witness very low conversion rates. No one is willing to sign up. You may realize that nobody wants what you are building, at least the way you presented it to the customer. Or it may happen that you witness spectacular conversion rates, but abysmal retention rates. If such things happen (they're bound to happen), you will see it coming and will be prepared for the next step—both intellectually and emotionally.

You will realize the fundamental flaw in your assumptions much sooner. Instead of spending months of additional work perfecting your product, thinking that the low conversion rates or the low engagement rates are due to lack of product features, you will consider the need to change your original strategy—pivot. But you will have recognized it much sooner, with a minimum waste of time and effort, and without beating yourself to the ground for your perceived failure. You will not place all your bets on your one idea, but with a scientific mindset, accept the reality and make amends accordingly. Instead of adding more features to your product, you will be open to accept that there is a more fundamental issue and redesign your experiments to test how you can overcome it.

Start with a new hypothesis, build a new MVP if needed, and validate its value and growth potential. A sign of your pivot being successful is that your activities will be significantly more productive after the pivot. You will feel that things are working well, instead of having to convince yourself and others about it.

This pivot can be in a variety of forms: a change in your growth model, a change in your market positioning, a change in your marketing strategy to target a different group of customers or a change in your business architecture and revenue models.

Stage Five: Optimize your key object with your customers

Once you validate your value and growth hypotheses with your customer, congratulations. Now you need to do some tuning up. Make your product easier for the customer to use.

Identify aspects of your MVP to optimize, so that you can drive up your core metrics. You start by filling in a set of baseline data from your first MVP. Conversion rates, engagement rates, churn rates, customer lifetime value, referral rates, and so on. However bad these numbers may be, this is your baseline from where you aspire to improve. You rigorously measure where you are right now, confronting the hard truths your assessments reveal. You experiment to learn how to move the numbers toward your ideal.

That you may make clear, objective decisions, it helps if you analyze your data in cohorts. These are groups of customers that come into contact with your product independently. For example, grouping all customers who registered with your product in May into one cohort, June into another, and so on. Introduce individual product improvements to these cohorts and analyze how that change affects the behavior of your cohorts. This strategy helps in eliminating interference from other factors that may have affected the results of your experiments, if you were not analyzing in cohorts but as gross numbers—which are the existing customers who may be resistant to change, ever-changing external market conditions, and such other potential factors that will reinforce your confirmation biases. If each independent cohort is exhibiting similar behavior to the change you are testing, you know, without a doubt, the change is solely responsible for the behavior.

Launch each additional feature as split test experiments. A split test experiment (also called A/B testing)[44] is when you offer two different versions of your product to two different sets of customers at the same time. By observing the change in behavior between the two groups, you can analyze the impact of the different variations. For example, if you want to test the impact of the design of your website's landing page on sign-ups, send the alternative version to 50 percent of your new customers and send the old version to the other 50 percent. To minimize interference, keep the content (wordings) of the website the same across both variations, only change the design. Simply track the number of sign-ups in both groups and you'll know which of the two designs is more effective. Split testing is routinely used in user experience research, but it's also a great tool for product development.

The combination of cohort analysis and split testing is a powerful tool for startups. It combines scientific rigor with agility. By carefully designing your experiments, you will be able to optimize your product, one feature at a time, one design change at a time. You are no longer speculating or whiteboard strategizing. You are optimizing and validating every new change with your real customers. It also reveals the validity of some of the basic assumptions you made about your product.

For example, if despite making loads of new product improvements, the ratio of free trials to purchase remains low, you will need to rethink your ground assumptions—your value hypothesis in this case. The customer is probably not seeing enough value in your product to warrant using the credit card. If such a situation occurs, go back and empathize with your customers. Talk to them, hold focus groups, understand the problem, and try to find avenues where the true value may lie. Brainstorm new ideas for product experiments that may have more impact.

Remember to set up experiments where you can analyze a clear cause-and-effect relation. Otherwise, you will never clearly know what effort led to the result you are seeing, and you will fumble around in the dark.

Tuning up your growth engine

Remember the growth hypothesis you validated at the beginning of your MVP testing phase? Now is the time to understand and rev up the engine that drives the growth of your business. In *The Lean Startup*, Eric Ries identifies three types of growth engines: sticky, viral, and paid. Refer to the book for an in-depth understanding about the growth engines. In summary:

If your product attracts and retains customers for the long term, then yours is a "**sticky growth engine**." eBay would be an example of a sticky growth engine. It operates on network effect and needs to retain its existing customers, while it adds new ones. It is likewise with enterprise software products that need customer lock-in with high switching costs. In such types of businesses, once a customer starts using your product, the expectation is that they will continue to do so. As long as the rate of new customer acquisition exceeds the churn rate (the ratio of new customers acquired to the loss of existing customers within a period of time is the "stickiness coefficient"), the business will grow. If you're adding new customers through ad buys, but consistently losing customers, you will find it very difficult to keep your stickiness coefficient greater than one. Your focus should rather be on improvising your product to increase retention rates.

If your product has a component of growth added within its very nature, then yours is a "**viral growth engine**." Facebook is perhaps the best example of a viral growth engine. In the early days, Facebook saw unprecedented growth. Every new Facebook user wanted their friends to use it so the user could build their own social network. Every new friend added more new friends and the process took on exponential growth. Product awareness spread similarly to a virus in an epidemic. Facebook did nothing to fuel growth and they could not even control it.

Growth happened automatically as a side effect of customers using the product. The "viral coefficient" measures how many new customers will use the product as a consequence of each new customer using it. If your business has a viral coefficient greater than one, it means that every new customer will add more than one new customer and your business will grow without any intervention from you. You must then focus on increasing the viral coefficient above all else. Work on removing any friction in the process of new customers signing up and recruiting more new customers. If Facebook had charged its customers, it would have impeded the growth of the platform. Instead, it monetized its customers' attention by bringing in advertisers to the platform.

If you are paying to grow your business, then yours is the "**paid growth engine.**" Every company that uses an outbound sales and marketing force is working over a paid growth engine. The only point to remember here is how much you are paying to acquire new customers—the cost per acquisition (CPA)—and what is the net "lifetime value" (LTV) of each customer. The margin between the LTV and the CPA, after deducting variable costs, is the marginal profit. Beware of a common danger— companies commonly believe that by a rapid ad push, a sudden marketing surge, or a publicity stunt, they can afford to lose money on each customer and make it up in volumes later on. Do you think this will make sense if the LTV never goes beyond the CPA?

Correctly identifying and validating your growth engine will help you direct your energies where it will be most effective in growing your business. Each engine requires a focus on unique metrics to evaluate success and design new experiments. It will tell you ahead in time if your business will continue to grow, or your growth engine will run out of steam.

More than one growth engine may apply to your business. You may expand your business through viral growth, but you may also need to operate with a high stickiness coefficient to sustain your growth and not fall into a downward spiral. Likewise, you may operate on a sticky growth engine, ensuring high customer retention, but also use the paid growth engine to attract new customers. Focus on one engine at a time, hypothesize on an engine that is most likely to work for your business, validate it, and only then move your focus on a second one.

Third Loop: Lean Scale-up

By the time you have iterated within the second loop, you will have got a fair idea about value-creating activities and those that are a form of waste. Your product is shaping up with every new optimization run. It is no longer an MVP but now is a product with features. It is getting better and better in quality and functionality. You have increased your customer base several-fold because of these iterations. You are already scaling up. However, your scaling-up exercise is limited to your niche, early-adopter group. After a while, you would have saturated this group of early adopters and you would see a need to expand to mainstream customers. This set of customers is far less forgiving, and to satisfy them, you will need to make tremendous amounts of effort.

How do you go about designing your product to match the needs of the mainstream customer? Do you now work rigorously at the back end, formulate and build all the features you foresee in the ideal version of your product and then go for a big bang release? You work for months on a new version of your product for mass market release. Your MVP activity has been a success. You have seen firsthand that your product is incredibly valuable to the customer, and you are convinced that the next version of your product will create an impact on the market. Expectations are sky high. So, you work toward creating that perfect, high-quality, superb version of your product.

The problem with this approach is that though you may satisfy your obsessive-compulsive self about the perfection levels of your product, you will spend precious time building multiple features into your product. Expenses will pile up, stress and doubt will build up, fear of how the market will react, and of potential failure will build up as time passes.

As your product becomes more complex, your team will face more challenges fixing the bugs. You might face technical roadblocks, more challenges, more conflicts. The more work you get done, the more problems you face. You may have to postpone your launch date. You are falling into the trap of your desire for a perfect product. Eric Ries calls it the "death spiral of large batches."

You started adding all your additional features with the assumption that they matter to your customer. But this is only speculation. Every additional feature is potentially a form of waste unless it's been validated with the customer. If you delay testing, it comes with a high cost in terms of learning and cycle times. You will only know for sure once your product is in the hands of your customer. Why invest so much upfront work on such assumptions while you can in truth test everything out with your real customers? You already have a platform for experimentation at your disposal. Use it by all means!

Stage Six: *Validate each additional feature of your product with your customer*

Start at Stage Zero—begin by gaining a fundamental understanding of this new set of customers. Now we are coming out of the niche group and focusing on mainstream thinking within your customer group. Give yourself a quick run-through of the first loop—diligently conduct a small set of semi-structured interviews, gather your insights, and use them to decide on initial features that may be more important to add to your product so that you can appeal to the mainstream customer. Skip the second loop and jump onto the third loop. Operating within this third loop will be quite similar to the second loop. You are treating your product as an MVP for the mainstream customer and building upon that. You are scaling up while sticking to the lean, agile approach you followed when developing your MVP. You can never assume which new features are of value to your customer. Formulate your hypotheses as you did earlier. For each additional feature you test, have your product development team design and run the experiments as quickly as possible, using the smallest batch size that can get the job done. By batch size, we mean releasing a smaller number of features every few days or weeks or months to a small set of customer cohorts. Instead of adding several extra features at one go. How does this help? Instead of learning how to build a product with a great number of features, you learn how to build a sustainable business within short learning cycle times.

Working in small batches may sound counterintuitive when you are scaling up. After all, working in larger batches improves efficiency. However, measuring your team's productivity in terms of how many extra features it can bring out within a period has no meaning if these extra features are not perceived as valuable by the customer.

Stage Seven: *Optimize and continuously improve your product*

Use the same metrics you used when optimizing your MVP to optimize your product. Instead of relying on gross metrics such as total customer number and total revenues, use your core metrics that highlight factors such as customer engagement, and optimize your product with the singular aim of maximizing these metrics. Use the cohort and split testing tools as before to observe true cause-and-effect relations between every new change and your customers' behavior.

Through these experiments, you are continuously improving your product, one step at a time. You have developed the ability to learn faster from customers, use it to your advantage even when scaling up.

Empathize with your customers and through occasional informal interactions, keep a tab on new business opportunities, innovating in existing and newer areas. By doing this, you are also in knowledge of your competitors—new entrants, copy-cats, fast followers. To overcome the commoditization of your product, remember to articulate WHY your company exists in the market and share that ethos with your customers as you grow. Let them know they are not just interacting with a lifeless product but with a group of people who share a similar worldview and belief system as them.

(*Simon Krystman, Susanna Nissar,* and *Saumita Banerjee*)

HOW TO FILL A HOL

THE KE

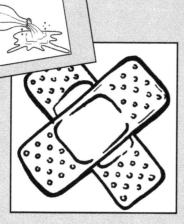

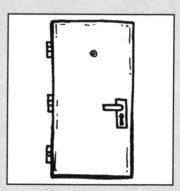

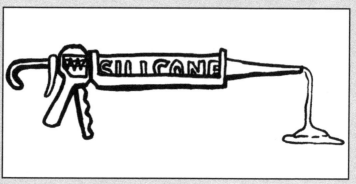

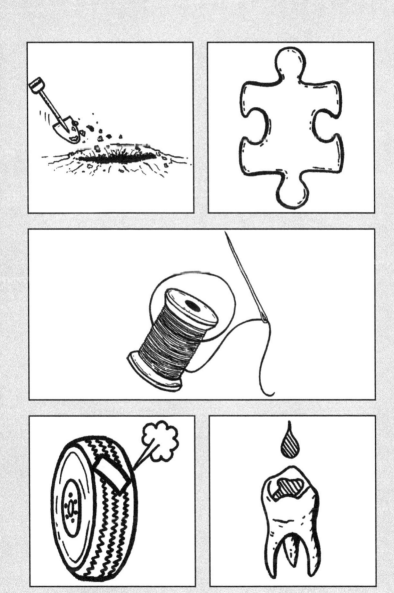

9
THE INNOVATOR'S BUSINESS CANVAS

An idea has many complements that make it a scalable business or project. A business model is no more than a representation of how an organization makes (or intends to make) money.[45] Creating your business model—a skeleton or a framework of your business before you jump on the operational side—is the step where the idea-to-startup transformation begins. Some entrepreneurs believe that a business model is only for medium or big businesses. Not only is this a myth but creating your business model is an essential step if you want to communicate your idea clearly to your founding team.

Is it applicable to any business or in any geography? The answer is YES. A business model is a frequently used and proven tool for businesses of any type, size, and geography.

Most big businesses use the Business Model Canvas (BM Canvas), a highly popular tool to visualize the framework of the business, highlighting the business structure with a detailed explanation of the operations and connections between all the wheels of the business. First proposed by Alexander Osterwalder, the BM Canvas has nine components:

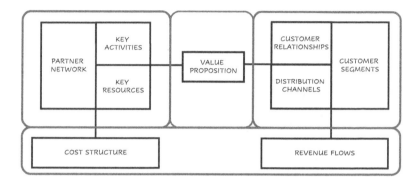

Figure 7: Use Alexander Osterwalder's Business Model Canvas to visualize the framework of your business. Used by big businesses, it highlights the structure of the business with a detailed explanation of the operations and connections between all its wheels.

As an entrepreneur, you may feel overwhelmed looking at the many components of the BM Canvas. You may wonder, "How am I going to fill all those blocks when I do not have enough clarity about so many aspects of my business at this moment?" This is a common observation for early-stage startups and a very valid one.

To address these concerns of early-stage entrepreneurs, adaptations of the BM Canvas have been proposed. The "Lean Canvas" is one such adaptation.[46]

Designed for agile startups, the Lean Canvas adapts the BM Canvas, a solution-focused model, for a problem-focused approach. Specially designed for entrepreneurs (rather than investors) it caters to the needs of startups focused on solving the problems of their customers.

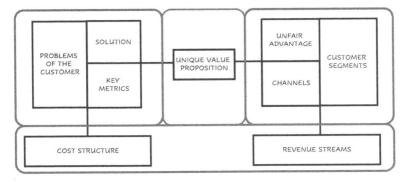

Figure 8· The Lean Canvas is an adaptation of the BM Canvas, specially designed for entrepreneurs. It caters to the needs of startups focused on solving the problems of their customers.

The Lean Canvas also has nine components but substitutes some blocks in the BM Canvas with some new ones. It starts with defining the problem and introduces a new term, "Unfair Advantage." Ash Maurya, the creator of Lean Canvas defines unfair advantage as something that cannot be copied or has a real competitive advantage. Entrepreneurs sometimes get confused with Unique Value Proposition (UVP) and Unfair Advantage. UVP is to capture the customer's attention whereas Unfair Advantage is to stop duplication of the idea.

Throughout this book, we have highlighted the importance of launching your product with your customer; a customer-centric approach. Empathizing with your customer at every step of idea and product development and continuously improving your product for them. How might a business-model framework look like, when you incorporate this customer-first philosophy into your business model?

The one essential question you asked yourself at the beginning of this book to understand your customer was: "Who is it for?"

This question, interestingly, forms the top right block in Osterwalder's BM Canvas, "customer segments." Instead of segmenting your customer into demographics, we are looking at them as real human beings—people with actual problems and needs that your business is attempting to address and solve.

This approach leads to a change of paradigm. Instead of asking at the end, "I have a great product and I need more people to buy it. I have a marketing problem," you will begin with, "What change do I seek to make?" Your WHY is now clearly articulated.

A customer-centric business plan makes the purpose and the WHY more specific, describing who and what it is for.

Seth Godin, in his book *This is Marketing*, divides the modern business plan into five sections[47]—"Truth," "Assertions," "Alternatives," "People," and "Money."

"Truth" is about the world as it is now; the state of the market we are entering, comprising needs, competitors, technologies, and market shares. The more specifically this truth is defined, the better. It is not a partisan view; it just states how things are.

"Assertions" are the changes you want to make happen. They are the impacts you want to have. You will present your product to the market and the market will respond in this way. Your arrival will change the market and the lives of people. How? You tell your story and create tension. This will form the heart of your business plan.

What if your assertions turn out to be inaccurate (and they will be)? You will miss budgets, deadlines, and sales. So, what will you do if that happens? What flexibility do you have in your solution? Your Plans B, C, and so on form your "Alternatives"—the several other hypotheses you will test on the way to building your business.

"People" is about customers and tribes. Who are the people you are serving? What are their attitudes, their worldviews, and their beliefs? Who is on your team? What are their attitudes, their worldviews, and their beliefs?

"Money" is about financial issues in all forms, which include needs, spend, profit & loss reports, cash-flow statements, balance sheets, margins, and exit strategies.

If we take these five sections and represent them in a BM Canvas-like model, it would look like a rather uncluttered version of it. We like to call it the Innovator's Canvas.

This Innovator's Canvas as a business model may not be popular with VCs, but it should help you and your team think through the hard issues more clearly. It is a merged representation of Seth Godin's business plan components and Osterwalder's BM Canvas.

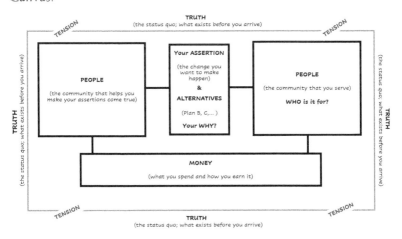

Figure 9: The Innovator's Canvas is a business-model framework incorporating the customer-first philosophy. A highly flexible model, it helps make the purpose and the WHY more specific. At its heart are "Assertions"—the changes you want to make happen, and "Alternatives"—the several other hypotheses you will test on the way to building your business, if your assertions turn out to be inaccurate (which they will).

Your business model does not represent your purpose or your mission. It's simply what you do—a clear description of WHO and WHAT it is for.

If your business model doesn't work, it doesn't mean your purpose or your WHY is doomed. It only means that you've ruled out one more route in your quest to matter.

Now you can explore another one.

(*Aditya Bhatnagar* and *Jean-Marie Buchilly*)

IV

SHOW YOURSELF

10
TELL YOUR STORY, SHARE YOUR ASSERTIONS, GET THEIR ATTENTION

When your product is ready to be shared with your customers, you can start to market it. You market it because you want to make change happen; you want to have an impact. Everything starts here with an assertion and a story; something that will challenge the status quo and create tension.

Real marketing is about sharing your assertions.

"You can't be seen until you learn to see" is the subtitle of a book written by Seth Godin. This book is about marketing; about the very essence of what marketing is. "Marketers don't use consumers to solve their company's problem; they use marketing to solve other people's problems," writes Seth Godin in his book *This is Marketing*.

Much too often, marketing is seen as this layer we put on things to make them shine.

This is not true. Marketing is the opposite of a varnish; it is the basis of a business.

Being an agent of change is being someone who brings a story to the scene, creates tension, and relieves it. The status quo doesn't shift because you are right. It shifts because of the tension you bring into your story.

You will get attention because you will deserve it. Because you will propose something new that has the power to challenge the way we do things.

It's not about you. It's about them. About the value and the benefits embedded in your assertion. About what is now possible because you spoke and exposed yourself.

Marketing is a promise. Not a promise about the specific performance of a product or a service. No, it's a promise about the fact that you care and share a worldview and a core belief with your audience.

That's why there is no mass marketing. Because marketing is an interesting conversation about a serious and specific topic and there is no chance that everybody cares about the one you chose to care about.

Your assertion is not for everybody.

How to get their attention

Seth Godin, in his book *Purple Cow: Transform Your Business by Being Remarkable*, introduces the term "attention marketing."[48] The book tells us that a close connection is needed between marketing and product for the latter to get attention.

If you have followed this book through, you are likely to have a very clear understanding of your customer, their worldviews, and their beliefs. You have empathized with them at every stage of developing your idea and know their persona (the factors which shape the character of your customer) very well.

A clear WHO helps you clearly identify and describe aspects of your product or service that resonate with your target customer. You share the core benefit of your product (the fundamental need that the customer satisfies after buying your product) in an uncluttered fashion. Instead of listing out the many features of your product, you communicate why you care to build your product and bring it to the market, and why your customer needs it. To take an example from Simon Sinek's *Start with Why*, instead of marketing a "5 GB MP3 player," Apple marketed "1,000 songs in your pocket," with a purpose to change the way their customer listened to their favorite songs when away from home.

Attention is the currency your customers subconsciously decide to spend based on the marketing communication of your product. If you can communicate clearly why your product will appeal to your customer, you will create a market pull, instead of needing to push your product.

Remember this: It's not about you. It's about them.

One of the fundamental frameworks to influence the customer's decision-making process is the 4P Framework—Product, Price, Place, Promotion.

- **Product**: A product has three layers—core product, generic product, and augmented product. The core benefit to the customer is provided by the core product or the first layer and to arrive at the actual product, it transits through certain steps like branding, features, quality. This gives the product the face and generic profile. After that, the guarantees, servicing, standards come under the augmented layer.

- **Price**: This is the value you aim to capture with your product. Price is one of the most influential factors and shapes your customer's perception of your company and your product.

- **Place**: Place is about the geographical placing of your product, and the channels (own sales, distributors, resellers, retailers) you are using to get to market, always keeping in mind your customers. London's been the financial capital of Europe before Brexit, but not every successful European fintech startup launched its product in London. For an online product, you narrow down your platform and social media channels to appeal to the culture and worldviews of your users and the place they come from.

- **Promotion**: This involves leveraging the right channels to reach your customers.

Here is a fictional example of a poor communication strategy: Take a SaaS-based startup trying to get attention for their digital learning and knowledge management product through print ads offering free trials for workers of a mechanical factory.

Breaking down the above example to the elements involved we have:

- "SaaS-based product"—the product
- "print ads"—the medium of communication
- "offering free trials"—the message of communication
- "for workers of a mechanical factory"—the WHO

A SaaS-based, digital product is directly being offered to factory workers, an unrelated segment presumably not too tech-savvy. In addition, the medium of communicating the message is print ads, again unrelated to the type of the product. What impact do you think this advertisement will have on the company and its product?

(*Jean-Marie Buchilly* and *Aditya Bhatnagar*)

Case Study: How to Get the Attention of Your First 10,000 Users

Yehoshua Zlotogorski is the co-founder and CEO of Alpe Audio. Alpe is an audio education platform (think Coursera meets podcasts) for young professionals who need to learn and master new topics but have a busy lifestyle. Alpe enables users to master topics from A–Z in the time they have—which is when they are "on the go"—commuting, running errands, or out for a jog.

The growth playbook for early-stage startups isn't well-known. There simply aren't many people who've done it. Sure, there are lots of product managers, growth managers, "gurus," and "ninjas" from all kinds of fantastic companies—Uber, Airbnb, Monday.com, Lemonade, and so on—but most likely they don't have relevant experience and advice for this stage, when you have no funds, no team, resources or simply users to do good A/B tests.

Yehoshua was bootstrapping growth, and neither had resources for paid advertising (also known as growth marketing) nor was a part of the "in" influencer crowds on social media. Despite his constraints, his aim was clear—he was looking at growing from 0 to 10,000 users within a span of 6 months.

Going from "zero to one" (or 0–1,000)

The goal at the beginning was very clear. It wasn't to grow top-line users. It was to iterate on the product and improve upon user retention metrics. It was about empathizing, validating, and optimizing an MVP-stage product. To do that, they had to find a benchmark for the metrics. After all, what is good retention, what is bad? If a user finished an entire course but then never returned for another one—is that good because they enjoyed the content or is that bad because they left the platform?

They used their own data and user interviews to measure a "successful" user and their "willingness to pay." The metrics they aimed for:

- 90-day retention: at least 30 percent
- Weekly Active Users (WAUs) logging in: about twice a week
- WAUs learning: about 50 minutes

This was a real challenge—they were bootstrapping, had little content or development resources and user expectations were higher than ever. They were also competing with podcasts which have an almost infinite amount of free to boot great content (this startup thing is a heavy lift).

To iterate and improve on the retention metrics, they needed a steady drip of users every week, so that they could test features, hear feedback, and improve their offering. This was their reason to grow at this stage. It wasn't about a big bump of users, rather it was about steadily growing weekly installs, which would drip down the funnel into their core learners—a much harder goal.

It's much easier to spend $500 on a one-time promo or giveaway to gain traffic. It's much harder to build a robust mechanism to acquire customers that works steadily and compounds over time. This is all that was needed to improve Alpe.

Between user #1 and user #1,000 there were two stages:

- Private beta: MVP: 0–400 users—seeing your product works (validation), getting some initial, raw feedback, and iterating to improve your value proposition (optimization).
- Product launch: 400–1,000 users—setting the foundations for growth.

Getting to 400 users

This was straightforward. Between a team of two co-founders and three interns, they spent hours on WhatsApp and Facebook finding 400 acquaintances who they thought were good testers. Their major hurdle at the beginning was the diffidence of reaching out to people and asking them to download and check out their app. Fortunately, they did not face any hard rejections. People were supportive and did not take offense from their "please download my app" message.

This set of people were their early testers, people they carefully followed up for feedback. This cohort is the one that provides the most feedback, and hence it's important to give enough time and attention to each one of them.

They didn't onboard all these users at once; they spread them out over four weeks. They manually dripped in the user growth because they wanted to iterate and measure improvements, and not overwhelm themselves.

The emotional challenge of showing your product (that barely works at this stage) to all people you know, such as your friends, family, and business contacts, can be quite intimidating. Your MVP becomes your representative, your emissary, to the world. When it is full of bugs, you feel that you are full of bugs. You identify yourself with your product and may find it uncomfortable showing a not-so-perfect version of yourself to all people in your circle. The feedback—especially the constructive criticism, can be emotionally draining. Prepare yourself for this.

Another strategy that worked

Student focus groups: They reached out to several professors/ innovation courses to pitch Alpe and while not all were interested, most were, and some were happy to assign Alpe as a research project for students. This gave them an immediate cohort of engaged "beta testers." Engaging 2–3 groups like this results in 60-70 users. While these weren't organic users per se, they provided valuable information and feedback.

What communities could be relevant to you?

From 400 to 1,000 users

Going from 400–1,000 is where things go beyond your circles. Now your focus is on finding your growth channels. Testing growth avenues to see what works and what doesn't. Now you need larger weekly cohorts. To analyze user journeys, funnels, retention, test features at a faster pace. You shift gears from qualitative analysis to quantitative.

There are certain things to do from day zero, preferably even before then if you can:

- **Set up social media presence for your company.** Facebook, Instagram, LinkedIn, Twitter, and so on.

- Spend a couple of hours researching **best practices on social media posting**. Not so much that you get frozen by perfectionism, not too little that your posts are ineffective. For example, you want to know that LinkedIn works best with both images and text, that adding 3–7 hashtags make a difference to visibility and that commenting on a post is better than sharing. Facebook is different—sharing is better than commenting and hashtags don't matter.

- **Start posting!** When you grow, people will look at your pages—the more legitimate and richer they are, the better. If they're empty, people won't convert.

- **Follow the right people.** Every space has influencers and thought leaders, and sub-communities on Slack, Reddit, and Discord. Join and follow them. Start seeing how the influencers think and what they post about. This will help you curate your feed for later with good relevant content and help you engage with the right people.

- **Find out where your users hang out online.** Sparktoro.com is a wonderful tool for this. Start getting acquainted with those places, whether it's TikTok, Facebook, Reddit, Chess.com, or specific forums.

- **Set up multiple users for the high-priority locations.** This sounds "bot-like" but it isn't. The idea isn't to spam, it is to:

  - Have different users so you can test different posts; not as your actual handle.

  - Interact with yourself to raise engagement—very important for early-stage startups when you don't have a brand. Humans are herd animals—we come to where the action is.

- **Build out your profiles' authenticity and functionality.** The point above is especially true for communities like Reddit and Quora, where you have to first contribute to other's answers before you can post your messages and get traction. So, start early and build useful profiles—this can often take a month or two of organic work.

- **Generate value on social media.** Start getting involved in conversations regarding your space on social media. By now you should be an expert in your space, doubly so if you're following the right accounts. Start generating value for users in whatever internet communities are relevant to you.

- There are some **other things to lay the groundwork for**— mainly Public Relations (PR), Search Engine Optimization (SEO), and App Store Optimization (ASO).

- **Give an engagement boost.** If possible, create a small group of "ringer" friends who are committed to engaging with each other's posts.

This might sound like a lot of things to do, and it is, but it's manageable. Set aside 30–60 minutes a day as your marketing foundations time. In that time get all of the above done—post, interact on social media, and track what's going on in your industry.

The growth effects of these start slow, especially if you're starting from a low base of users, but they compound over time.

Bootstrapping to 10,000 users: Choosing the right marketing distribution channels

Once you've figured out where your users are and established a social media presence, it's time to figure out your best channels for customer acquisition. There are many, many channels. Most won't work. It's up to you to test them and find what works for you. The team at Alpe followed the "bullseye" framework laid out in Gabriel Weinberg and Justin Mares' book *Traction*,[49] a great book on—well, traction.

Briefly, the bullseye framework states you start at the outer edges of your target by listing all the channels you could use, then you test them a few at a time and see what works. The bullseye is when you find out what works—double down on that.

Here's the list that was built and tested:

- app store advertising (iOS/Android)
- Google AdWords
- paid social media—Facebook, Twitter, LinkedIn, TikTok, Instagram
- organic social media
- Reddit and Quora
- audio advertising—Podcasts and Spotify
- sponsoring newsletters
- direct mailing lists
- direct physical mail—yup, still a thing
- community partnerships
- community outreach
- "earned PR"—being hosted on podcasts/newsletters
- blogs

Each of these have their quirks and features. For example, some are more scalable, some are cheaper, some require more upfront cost (time or effort) or have bad tracking, some require connections.

Choose and test these channels with a clear goal in mind. For Alpe, it was to hit 10 percent weekly growth for several months at the least, for a tiny budget of $75–100 a week.

Start where you're comfortable and where you have a gut feeling you'll see the most success. Each of these channels requires effort. You need to study up on best practices, read blogs, reach out to different experts. Try to minimize the learning curve—you've got enough on your plate as it is and you've probably got a decent gut feeling on where your users are hanging out.

Speak to industry experts. See what they think. The Alpe team spoke to friends who run growth at companies like Lemonade, JoyTunes, Monday.com, and Uber. From them they collected off-piste nuggets, like the minimum budget for a successful Facebook campaign is at least $15,000, that Twitter is lackluster for direct advertising and that podcasts lack tracking.

They also made some interesting observations:

- In the app stores, ads for specific sections in the app (e.g., specific courses) brought users with higher intent who converted better.
- Ads should address the user and NOT the product. Instead of "Audio courses platform," use "Become a lifelong learner." Remember? It's not about you, it's about them.

Learning cycle

Start by trialing 2–3 different channels every two weeks. Study the channels in advance so that a test could run for a whole two weeks before deciding whether to dump or keep on trialing. A typical process can look like this:

- Start trials on platforms you know best and have performed all your research on.

- Dive deep into the next 2–4 channels and decide which to trial next and how.

- Test each channel for two weeks, analyze the data, decide whether to cut or tweak, and keep on trialing.

- Following two more weeks of the trial, analyze cohort retention to see if the users brought in were high quality or not (or use some other way to test your trial results).

It will take you about 6–8 weeks to trial most of the distribution channels. Some platforms may require longer to trial:

- Facebook and Google require running different tests so that their algorithms can kick in and you can get a sense of better copy.

- Newsletter and podcast ad placements must be booked in advance.

- Community partnerships take time to build and launch (for example, many have newsletters/digests that go out every so often).

So, what worked for Alpe?

App store advertising

This worked very well for Alpe—in both iOS and Google Play. The iOS store is a good place to start if you're looking for Apple users. Prices were relatively low, and efficacy was higher than social media, but the cost limit per user put a cap on the number of users Apple could bring each day.

If your users are on Android, Google is the best platform for advertising—by a big margin. The global reach and targeting enabled a much lower cost per user without giving up on high intent users.

In Google Play Store users install apps they see while browsing the play store, whereas in Apple Play Store users search for a specific app and install it. Keep in mind this difference in user behaviors when running your ads.

Organic and paid social media

For Alpe, Facebook turned out to be an expensive game. Twitter's ad platform proved hard to use and hard to iterate upon. While they generated hundreds—even thousands of impressions monthly over social media, they failed to achieve meaningful growth metrics. The team couldn't quite figure out the organic side of Reddit and Quora and couldn't drive great engagement. These are experiences specific to the Alpe team and yours can be very different.

Podcasts and Spotify

Since Alpe Audio is audio-based education, this would seem a natural fit. However, the podcasting advertising ecosystem is still nascent in a few key ways that can be challenging for an early-stage startup:

- There's no "ad network" that can guarantee good targeting; much of the targeting needs to be done by choosing the right podcast. Spotify's ad network is still very early and not available globally.

- Podcasting is bifurcated. The successful podcasts can go above your budget while the smaller podcasts have a much smaller reach and are much harder to find.

- In podcasting there is a lead time to close a deal, create the copy and then make it go live at a future time.
- Creating new ad copy requires resources.
- Worse tracking. It's hard enough to understand the efficacy of dollars spent on the best-in-class platforms like Facebook and Google. For podcasts, this can be much, much harder.

Seeing as they were in the testing phase to understand what could give the best return on investment, podcasts did not seem worth the effort.

Community outreach

Engaging in forums that were relevant to Alpe's courses proved highly effective. While this required more upfront effort and wasn't as scalable, the users that came from this organic "guerilla" marketing were much higher quality.

For example, Facebook groups or Slack channels around product management proved great places to show the value of Alpe's Product Management course. It's important to note that this isn't about spamming users in those communities or being blatantly self-promotional. It's about adding value with high-quality content. Generate value for people to be interested in what you have to say. How can you create value? Be interesting, educate on your space, have opinions, tell them things that you know they don't.

Earned PR (leveraging existing community distribution)

While probably the least scalable of all the channels, being able to hop on board existing communities' distribution channels is powerful. This includes being hosted on podcasts, added to newsletters, or invited to panels. It's not very scalable since it requires dedicated outreach and quality content, but if you find the right communities, it can be powerful.

Follow and engage with relevant communities for several months and when the time is right, reach out to community leaders and form meaningful collaborations.

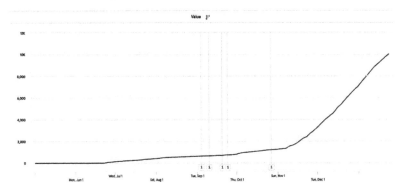

Figure 10: For an entrepreneur with scarce resources, everything is done under constraints, and so everything is a trade-off. Running a systematic, iterative process focused on identifying what works and what doesn't, and doubling down on that which works, is the mantra for successfully growing your venture from zero to 10,000 users.

Bringing it all together

For an entrepreneur with no resources, everything is done under constraints, and so everything is a trade-off. Make those trade-offs—you can't have it all. You might have to acquire fewer users if your quality bar is very high, simply because of the cost of direct advertising.

Use the bullseye model: This model helps you sketch out more distribution channels than you might originally think are available to you, as well as a plan of action on how to iterate through them and find the bullseye channel that will work best for you.

Receiving quick quality feedback and iterating quickly is

critical for success. Getting things done within a week or two is challenging and so you need to develop a core group of users and partners you can trust and rely on to provide you with quality feedback—fast.

Run a systematic process. Trust your gut, but also trust the process. The entrepreneurship game is tough: we fail at more things than we succeed at. Put a system in place to make sure you're running smoothly and quickly even when the going gets tough.

(Yehoshua Zlotogorski)

11
BRANDING AND BRAND
MARKETING

At the concept stage, your fresh ideas have no financial value, shape, or direction. They are abstract and amorphous, feeling their way into the world. Think of your new ideas in terms of the time between birth and puberty—human beings and the ideas we have go through similar developmental stages.

In Philip Pullman's "His Dark Materials" series of novels set in an alternative universe,[50] every human character has an external animal persona—called a daemon—that lives symbiotically attached to its host, displaying the person's personality and inner-life emotions. Throughout their early years, children's daemons change often, in line with their personal development—mentally, physically and spiritually. This is a time of experimentation, play and discovery. When children reach adolescence—and only then—their animal daemon becomes fixed, remaining so for the rest of their lives.

Relating this to new business ideas, fresh concepts are not mature—they are subject to growth in many directions, influenced by data, experience, prelaunch feedback, research, further related ideas, and so on. While an idea is in development, its daemon is constantly changing as the concept takes shape. As the idea evolves, it forms into a more concrete innovation that can be tested in the marketplace with prelaunch early-adopter customers, using agile marketing to adjust the demographic and interest groups that are to be approached for their feedback. Only when the idea achieves an exact market-fit validation can it be deemed to have a value that can attract further customers. Once this validation is secured, the idea is mature enough for its daemon to be fixed.

At this stage of innovation—when the idea has found a viable market, where its consequent products and services solve consumer problems, and where it addresses needs and reduces pain points—the concept's persona (its daemon) is now fixed, for the lifetime of the idea and its applications. The innovation now has sufficient concrete form for it to be ready for its next phase—developing a brand. It is only when the innovation is proven to meet a market need within a viable, commercial niche—backed up with data, such as prelaunch orders—that time and resources should be spent on branding that matches the expectations of customers who are keen to purchase your products and services.

Lester Wunderman, the father of direct marketing, was the first to describe the difference between brand marketing and direct marketing.

Direct marketing is action oriented. It is measured.

Brand marketing is culturally oriented. It can't be measured.

Direct marketing will lead to orders and brand marketing will change the culture.

And here comes the powerful question Seth Godin asks all of

us: "If you could patiently invest more time and money in putting the story of your brand in the world, how would you do it?"[47]

Should you over-invest in the location of your business, design of your packaging, the way your team interacts with customers? Or increase your spending on R&D? Or go back to school, learn and improve your craft?

Seth doesn't give us the answer (because there is none) but leaves us with this advice about brand marketing: "You definitely, certainly, and surely don't have enough time and money to build a brand for everyone. You can't. Don't try. Be specific. Be very specific."[47]

And that's when all the pieces of the puzzle come together. Build your brand, keeping that specific set of people in mind and overdo your brand marketing. Make it so much a part of their lives that every time they see any of you, they should be able to make a smart guess about all of you. Because you now have a brand that embodies everything you are, from your beliefs to the way you behave every day.

(*Christopher Norris* and *Jean-Marie Buchilly*)

V

SUSTAIN AND THRIVE

12
CREATE VALUABLE
INTELLECTUAL PROPERTY

It's a mistake that starts with the best of intentions. Business owners rush to put in their patent applications, thinking the sooner the submission the better. So that your competition can't just come in and steal your idea. Turns out it's not that easy. Because if you start the process too early, you are putting the cart before the horse. You'll still be moving forward, but you might be throwing good money after bad, modifying your patent application, as your technology takes shape and becomes more fully formed. The worst-case scenario being that you blow a hole in your budget, and you still don't have the protection you need.

Even worse, you might give your competition valuable information to catch up with you even more quickly.

Meanwhile, you may have good intellectual property (IP) lying around gathering dust, without you having realized its true value yet.

So how does one approach this problem? Look at your company as you would look at yourself. What are your unique skills and talents that contribute to your success, that are valuable to the world? Similarly, what are the valuable IP assets of your company that make (or will make) it truly valuable in the market? Put your money only on those.

Don't ask if what you have is patentable. Ask what it is with you that is valuable, that can be leveraged to maximize your company's worth.

Create a plan to protect your innovation, your technology, your trade secrets. Attach a value to it. Filing a patent application is not always the only way to go if you want to protect your IP. Most people think that protecting your IP means filing a patent application and having everyone onboard sign the right agreements.

This may be the right way, but it is not the only way. You can create processes to ensure your IP stays protected, without having to spend a dime on IP protection.

And then, only if you HAVE to, identify the exact moment when your technology is formed enough to put through the patent application. Not a moment before. This is what is the Tipping Point. The result will be a more aligned patent that'll have more chances to increase the value of your protection, at the lowest possible cost.

Instead of focusing on filing your first patent(s), build a clear IP strategy—a framework for making decisions about how you will play the game of IP, in alignment with your business strategy.

The value of IP associated with inventions and brands, customer data and software continue to grow, as businesses increasingly depend on innovation and creativity to compete.

Your IP strategy framework

IP "protection" does not just happen. Your IP strategy framework needs to cover multiple components so that you ensure you identify your most valuable IP, protect it, and leverage it to maximize your company's worth. It typically includes the components shown in the figure.

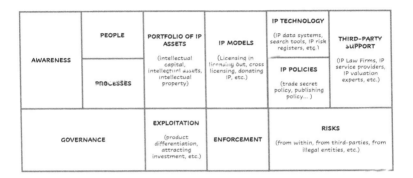

Figure 11: A well thought out IP strategy framework covers multiple components to ensure you identify your most valuable IP, protect it, and leverage it to maximize your company's worth.

Awareness:

Don't assume that everyone in your team knows what IP is, what information needs to be protected, and what they can share with others. They might feel excited to share too much of it over social media or tell a curious acquaintance much of what goes on in the company.

Make yourself and your team aware of what is meant by "intellectual property" and "proprietary information."

People:

Decide who in your team is to be included in your IP-related discussions and decisions. Minimize the number of people who have access to hypersensitive information.

Processes:

An IP process may be seen as an agreement to do certain things in a certain way. IP processes are like the memory of the organization, and without them, a lot of effort can be wasted, and the same mistakes can be repeated.

Portfolio of IP assets:

This is the list of all sensitive information in your business. Think about it this way: what information, if stolen or lost, would cause significant damage to your business? These are your intangible assets.

Intangible assets may be broken down into three categories:

- **Intellectual capital**: The knowledge and know-how, skills, competencies, and experiences of your people.

- **Intellectual assets**: These include everything documented manually or automatically within your company. Business plans, meeting minutes, supplier lists, customer details, process descriptions, product specifications, test scripts, test data, all fall into this important sub-category.

- **Intellectual property**: There are multiple regimes of intellectual property: patents, trademarks, designs, domain names, copyright, and trade secrets.

Managing your IP portfolio means understanding your IP assets, and what new IP assets should be created going forward to protect your company's innovation and creativity. Set time aside to regularly review your IP assets, align your IP portfolio to meet your business objectives, and avoid unnecessary costs. Where appropriate, it may mean trimming or monetizing redundant or non-core IP within your portfolio.

IP technology:

Evaluate if and how you can use technology (e.g., IP data systems, search tools, and IP risk registers) to help with IP management.

IP policies:

A policy statement is an organization-level document that prescribes acceptable methods or behaviors. Your IP-related policies may cover topics like:

- open-source software policy
- inventor reward and recognition policy
- trade secret policy
- publication policy

Third-party support:

There are entities in the IP sector offering products and services to help you with your IP issues. These include IP law firms, IP service providers, IP brokers, IP valuation experts, and IP insurance providers.

Determine which entities should become part of your third-party IP support network and how you can manage these relationships going forward.

Enforcement:

Not allowing others to use or commercialize your IP-protected innovations and creativity is IP enforcement. This can be done through civil, administrative, and penal measures aimed at preventing the unauthorized use of IP, sanctioning such use, and providing remedies to IP right holders for the damage caused by such unauthorized use.

Exploitation:

IP can be exploited in various ways and this is not just commercial or financial exploitation. Explore how your business can leverage IP to add value in the broadest sense. A variety of different ways include freedom to operate; product differentiation; revenue generation; tax benefits; cost advantage; commercial influence; enabling a new technology; attracting investment; enhancing reputation.

IP models:

No entity is an island. It interacts with third parties such as suppliers, customers, and partners. The nature of your relationship with these third parties will differ from one to another. Some of these relationships will be calm and some will be turbulent from an IP perspective. Leverage IP models such as IP licensing in, IP licensing out, IP cross-licensing, donating IP, leveraging interoperability standards, embracing open-source software, creative commons, leveraging platforms, working with a developer community, industry–academia collaboration, and outsourcing research and development to maintain relationships with third parties.

Clarify which IP models your company will embrace, for a rationale perspective, and which IP models you will try to avoid like the plague

Risks:

Companies face a multitude of IP-related risks that need to be understood and mitigated. IP risks can come from within the company (for example, employee theft or simply poor decision-making by employees) from competitors, from third parties—such as IP-holding companies, patent-assertion entities, and non-practicing entities—and from illegal entities, such as hackers and counterfeiters.[51]

Governance:

Define the rules of decision-making within your IP function. Ideally, the process should distinguish between strategic and tactical decisions.

The output

One fundamental question about an IP strategy is, "Where is the balance between simplicity and complexity?" On the one hand, you want the IP strategy to be easy to understand, communicate and provide clear direction. On the other hand, you want it to address everything. The IP strategy will also vary depending on whether the company is a startup, a scale-up, or an established player in its particular sector.

Your IP strategy will be critical to the success of your business and needs to be taken seriously. Be careful, don't create worthless IP. Don't file a patent only to prepare for your future investor meetings, for that one slide in your pitch deck that says "we have X patents." Don't rush to file your patent. The worst that can happen when delaying your filing is that you will end up with a better patent.

(*Donal O'Connell* and *Ilanit Appelfeld*)

13
NEED OUTSIDE MONEY?

Bootstrapping is about growing organically and reinvesting your profits into expansion activities. Funding from external sources is like injecting supplements to boost growth and expand much faster. Not all businesses can rely on organic growth, and most founders aspire to secure huge funds ahead of time to grow and sustain in the longer run.

Too many founders start their journey with the sole aim of securing big funding. They present their raw idea to various forums hoping to gain their first million-dollar break. Instead of believing in their idea and putting their skin in the game, they want other people to place the bet for them. They end up spending too much of their time and effort trying to attract investors, instead of acting on their idea. Even if their idea is promising and an investor takes a punt on the idea, the progression of the idea into a product happens with the investors in mind—working out how to impress them. Any investor who has put their money into your idea operates with a singular intention of getting high returns on their investment. Their primary agenda is to make money, not to make the customer happy. So, this leads to a disconnect that inevitably leads to various complications.

The success formula for a startup is in its potential to impact the lives of its customers and change the status quo. If you can demonstrate this core characteristic, I can say without a doubt that external funding will be much easier for you.

Most of what we discuss here is common knowledge; the figure below gives a fairly comprehensive list.

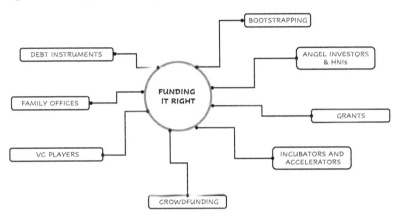

Figure 12: Where do you find the money? For early-stage startups, apart from bootstrapping, there are several avenues for raising funds. Carefully weigh your pros and cons to decide how important outside funding is to you.

For early-stage startups, apart from bootstrapping by the founders, angel investors and high net worth individuals (HNIs) are the ones who play key roles in funding. Some successful entrepreneurs transition into angel investors. Since they have been in your shoes earlier, there will be a lot you can learn from partnering with such entrepreneurs. HNIs who are not part of a VC network tend to invest in startups via crowdfunding platforms. Accelerator programs also help businesses raise equity in the early stages and provide mentoring advice and network.

VC players and family offices play key roles in Series A and B rounds. Angels and VCs have much higher risk appetites and so are one of the most preferred options for startup founders. They come in at stages when your business has still not achieved a product–market fit. They are ready to bet on the uncertainty. Besides infusing capital into your business, they also provide advice on steering the business.

Raising equity capital is like getting married; you have to have a good feeling about the compatibility in the long run. You will have to work with your partners and your relationship with them will make a big difference.

For companies with a ready playbook, progressing rapidly in terms of growth and revenues, there are venture debt funds that invest without collaterals. Finally, you have the good old option of raising funds through bank loans and other debt instruments.

The decision to stay bootstrapped or to raise outside funding is an important one for you to make. Carefully weigh your pros and cons, use the decision-making framework we discussed in Chapter 3 to decide how important outside funding is. Though it is easy to think that a funding boost is a sure-shot way to succeed, this isn't always true. Remember that too large a budget can be a harmful proposition. Countless dotcom failures attest to this. For a startup environment, scarcity and constraints are the rules of the game. These two elements can counterintuitively boost creativity.

Independent authority—absolute autonomy—is another important attribute essential to a startup when developing and marketing new products. You need to swiftly conceive and execute your experiments without having to gain approvals every time. If your investor does not agree with your approach of lean scale-up, you may have to change your ways and take steps that you may not feel comfortable executing. Making decisions under pressure affects the quality of the outcome. Carefully read the term sheet before signing your funding agreement.

Success in fundraising can bring you sudden fame and recognition in the public domain. When that happens, you become a public figure, and your successes and failures get carefully scrutinized. The cost of failure increases exponentially. Fear of failure is always there, even when you are the only one who knows about the problems of your business; when you are famous that fear takes on an extreme version. Everyone knows about the problems of your business; when you fail, everybody knows about it. Everybody is ready to judge you. This can be a very stressful situation. Prepare yourself for such eventualities. Obscurity can be good for a startup; too much attention can sometimes become a reason for failure. In such situations, build the courage to ignore your fears; focus on your customers instead of focusing on the words of those on the other side of the fence.

(Saumita Banerjee)

14
REMARKABLE OR INVISIBLE?

Aluwani Nemukula, an agricultural scientist by training, transitioned from an academic career into entrepreneurship about five years ago. He entered the business of farming with no training and no experience whatsoever. His goal at that time was just to make enough extra money. Like a true hustler, he became self-taught in every sense of the word. With no shortcuts and no handouts, he's a first-generation farmer.

In the beginning, he was doing everything, like every farmer around. Each planting season would start with land preparation, planting, anticipating weather cycles, crop protection, and finally harvest. Then came the battle of getting his produce to the markets and retail stores—only to find that he had made just enough to pay for the overheads. No profits, and then the cycle began again.

After a few cycles, he caught himself, literally scratching his head and kicking the ground, "Why am I doing this?" He hadn't realized until then that he was stuck, mired in a highly competitive business where every farmer around him was equally broke; there was no disparity. Luckily for him, his inner voice would not make peace with the situation. This could not be it. There had to be more. He didn't give up; instead, he began searching for ways to make his business proposition stand out. He began searching for his opportunity, for his WHY.

He started talking to his future customers—friends, family, and acquaintances—observing their pain points. He saw a demand for affordable vegetables in most households. He thought, how about growing one's own fresh vegetables anywhere, with less water and no space constraints? His scientific and innovative brain kicked in. After several iterations, he came up with a design idea for a portable vegetable growing product suitable for peri-urban farming.

It was a brilliant idea. An idea he was passionate about, an idea that fit his area of expertise, and an idea that served a bigger purpose—transforming the food system. Food security is one of the topical issues in South Africa, Aluwani's home country. His idea had the potential to fortify food security and build strong and sustainable livelihoods, while also solving the problems of rising food prices and market entry for subsistence farmers. Turning conventional methods of growing food crops into low-cost, high returns, and extremely efficient patented vegetable grower products. Most incredibly, each vegetable grower achieves all this in less than a 7 square feet space, which significantly reduces the carbon footprint required to grow food in large arable lands. He had found his WHY.

He began working on his idea to build his first MVP. Financial and human capital were readily sourced. He secured partners for IP and marketing. He onboarded design engineers and a molding company to take care of the technical drawings and manufacturing of the prototype.

Figure 13: After trying his hands at conventional farming, Aluwani Nemukula found an opportunity in peri-urban farming, with a low-cost, high return, and extremely efficient portable vegetable grower product. The patented VegiGrower™ enables one to grow their own fresh vegetables anywhere, with less water and no space constraints, addressing an unmet need for affordable vegetables.

Remember, human beings run businesses and customers often buy into the people in the business. He identified and understood his customer base and built his business by placing his customer at the center. Their worldviews, their status, their beliefs. He communicated his purpose clearly to them. This worked well for his business and the rest is history.

Aluwani saw an opportunity and seized it with an innovative solution. His business is now fighting the food security problem with actual solutions. The portable grower sales were so successful that it became a boom—he started enjoying incredible revenue numbers every month. Over the years he has diversified into other avenues like specialty crops, free-range poultry, honey, and has recently launched an agritech training center.

Aluwani says, "When I look back, I honestly owe much of the business success to taking an idea or opportunity and flipping it one step at a time. I truly believe it's a blessing to start from scratch because then you can build it up yourself. This way, you can stand out from the competition and develop more resilience I do not have any startup advice that is cast in stone because every business is different. But I would suggest that, if you want to stay in business and ahead of the crowd, find your unique proposition and run with it. Do not obsess so much about operating at scale. You must just innovate to take your business to the next level."

No doubt, it feels nice to be inspired by a business idea. It feels even nicer to be inspired by your work. But the core of any business is to SELL. In a world in which the vast majority of startups do not see the light of day and many entrepreneurs settle for the status quo, it is not enough to just feel safe and return home "fulfilled."

Building a successful business from scratch is difficult, and it does not happen overnight. It is a daunting task. But if you develop the resilience of working on your unique vision, mobilizing the right resources, and standing out from the crowd, you can certainly build the empire of your wildest dreams.

To do this, you have to look at your competition like a 100-meter sprint in the Olympics. Everyone in the race is gunning for the same ultimate prize—the gold medal—however only one of the elite athletes clinches the gold medal. But what everyone fails to realize is that the race itself is NOT won on race day. Elite athletes differentiate themselves by displaying what is called "creative monopoly." They work on their unique strength for hours, days, and weeks on end. And if you ask them, they'll tell you that talent is not enough. They just find their edge and use it to their advantage, against everyone else. Competition in business is no different. You must stand out from the crowd!

If your business offering has no meaningful differentiation, it will not stand out—and that means no profits. It will be a struggle for survival. So why do entrepreneurs find themselves trapped in competition? Our society has internalized competition as something healthy, but the more we compete, the less we gain— unless we stand out from the rest, like in the Olympics.

Seeing your business idea take shape and become a reality is both a humbling experience and a tremendous responsibility. In life and business, it is possible to make a good living doing exactly what you love to do. So, don't put this book down until you fuel your innovative idea. This matters the most. As for Aluwani and his team, they will not stop; opening a retail store is the next target. Until that happens, he's not tapping out.

(Aluwani Nemukula)

15
FEARLESS INNOVATION

Massimo Scalzo, an Italian entrepreneur, founded a technology startup. Within three years he made it such a remarkable success that it was bought out by a global giant in the information technology industry, awarding considerable dividends to him and the people who worked with him.

I asked him how he succeeded in bringing about such a quick turnaround? He said, "I'm sure the reason it ended well is that we had something to sell, which was sought after by the market. I'm also convinced that a big reason it ended well is because of the people with me. PEOPLE. That is essential for a startup."

He went on to explain, "As the CEO, I created the culture and values of the company, first thing with the right people. I always hired for human qualities first, then for skills. Hire for values, for who they are, not just for skills or worse for diplomas and qualifications. Look for the human qualities in people, and their ability to reflect those qualities within the company. I'm convinced that the more people with healthy beliefs and habits you have in your company, the greater and stronger is your company.

"I remember spending my days sending good vibes. By speaking, educating, writing, transforming back-end based companies into customer-centric enterprises, taking into due consideration the HUMAN SIDE. By creating a cozy and relaxed atmosphere. Even the interior design of the company reflected our culture. It was a sort of office that's difficult to leave when 5 o'clock rolls around. Everything stood as a defense against workplace anxiety and restrictions. That's how I like to think of a workplace, and that's how our workplace was.

"The environment naturally led to a sense of autonomy and pride among the staff. Every collaborator turned into a roving leader."

Building a culture of fearless innovation is about making the intangible, tangible, and actionable. An innovation culture is not in place because we declare it is, but because we behave accordingly. The value of an innovation culture is about its outcomes. It is about visualizing what fearless innovation will look like, and then taking steps toward making that vision a reality.

Where fearless innovation reigns, we observe the following impacts:

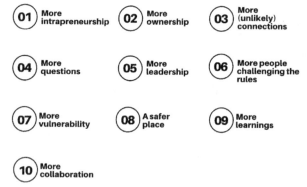

Figure 14: An innovation culture is not in place because we declare it is, but because we behave accordingly. The value of an innovation culture is about its outcomes. It is about visualizing what fearless innovation will look like, and then taking steps toward making that vision a reality. Where fearless innovation reigns, a number of impacts can be observed as shown here.

1. More intrapreneurship

We all have our worldviews. We all have our beliefs. We all see the world a certain way.

Intrapreneurs change the system from within. They act on the way they see the world and lead the change that they want to make happen. They use the organization, and its assets to make their idea come true.

At the first glance, it could seem easier to be an intrapreneur than an entrepreneur. These two, in reality, are very different. Intrapreneurs don't put their money at stake, though they put everything else. Their passion. Their energy. Their time. And sometimes even their job.

Being an intrapreneur and leading such a change requires sacrifices. It takes time and energy. It's an emotional rollercoaster, as people will go through moments of euphoria and discouragement. It can even put their job at risk. Anyway, this is the price to pay to build an organization they belong to and in which they can be their true and entire self. And not one in which they would only fit.

The book to dig deeper: *The Intrapreneur: Confessions of a corporate insurgent* by Gib Bulloch.[52]

2. More ownership

A job description typically describes the official roles and responsibilities of the job and a list of qualifications needed to perform it. We expect that the best candidate will be the one who best meets these requirements. There will be loads of applicants who fit the criteria. How will you decide which of them is the right fit?

What the typical job description does not mention is the

impact the candidate can (and will) have on the organization. Ownership is all about the impact we want to have. When you offer them something bigger than just their job, you attract the right kind. The kind whose belief and worldview match yours. The kind who are already motivated. A person who will work hard to look for innovative solutions, not for your company, but themselves. They will operate with a high level of ownership.

Most of the time, we have an opinion. We react to something based on our worldview and beliefs. Ownership is low.

Sometimes we take the lead. We make an assertion based on our worldview and beliefs. Ownership is high.

The safer the place, the higher is the level of ownership and the number of assertions. Because taking ownership requires both self-confidence and trust in the system (e.g., organization, community, or group) as people who take ownership and responsibility expose their true selves.

Ownership is about taking initiatives and making decisions considering the impact it could have on the organization instead of the internal rules and the risk to be sanctioned.

This is perfectly summarized in this quote: *"It is better to ask for forgiveness than permission."*

Here's yet another quote from Seth Godin that best describes ownership in a few words: *"No one is going to pick you. Pick yourself."*[53] The right fit, the right people for your organization, are the ones who already have the tendency to pick themselves. They do not wait for others to tell them what to do and how to do it. They'd rather pick the work themselves and start doing it. And the right culture is the one that enables and empowers them to exercise this tendency.

The book to dig deeper: *Extreme Ownership (How US Navy SEALs Lead and Win)* by Jocko Willink and Leif Babin.[54]

3. More (unlikely) connections

"Unlikely connections" are the two words that best describe innovation.

Innovations don't just come from nowhere. They result from combining and connecting existing ideas and concepts to make something new. And if these ideas and concepts have nothing to do with each other, then we have an unlikely connection. For example, you might be able to take a concept from outside your industry to make a breakthrough innovation happen.

Unlikely connections provide a genuine feeling of creation at the very moment we identify the possibility of a connection. It's like endorphin for a runner.

Actively seeking these unlikely connections requires a specific mindset, a broad general knowledge (range), and a lot of imagination, creativity, and an open mind.

The book to dig deeper: *Range: Why Generalists Triumph in a Specialized World* by David Epstein.[55]

4. More questions

We ask questions to:

- learn something
- challenge a vision
- show that we disagree

- show that we agree
- play for time
- show our interest
- observe reactions
- force people to share their (true) beliefs
- convince
- make people think
- help people imagine a different future (the "what if" and "how might we" questions)
- understand the big picture
- connect the dots

We think that people expect brilliant answers from us.

In reality, our best contribution is asking better questions.

Ask questions: to other leaders, to your colleagues, to your teams. Ask questions to anyone regardless of their roles and responsibilities and their position in the organizational chart.

The book to dig deeper: *The Coaching Habit: Say Less, Ask More & Change the Way You Lead Forever* by Michael Bungay Stanier.[56]

5. More leadership

Leaders have ideas. Leadership is an art.

Leadership being an art means it is not a skill. It requires mastering plenty of skills to master an art.

"The first responsibility of a leader is to define reality. The last is to say thank you. In between the two, the leader must become a servant and a debtor.

That sums up the progress of an artful leader," says Max De Pree, American businessman and bestseller author in his book *Leadership is an Art.*[57]

Leaders must provide and maintain momentum.

Leaders are also responsible for future leadership.

Leaders owe the corporation rationality.

Leaders owe people space: space in the sense of freedom.

Leaders are responsible for effectiveness by enabling others to reach their potential. By encouraging roving leadership, creating a purpose, sharing ownership of problems, and inspiring people in your organization to find their voice, lead, and take charge. Roving leadership practiced freely and openly is the vehicle we can use to reach our potential.

Leaders see opportunity where others see trouble.

"We must become, for all who are involved, a place of realized potential," says De Pree.

Leaders, in a special way, are liable for what happens in the future, rather than what is happening day-to-day. The liability is difficult to measure, and thus the performance of leaders is difficult to measure.

The book to dig deeper: *Leadership is an Art* by Max De Pree.

6. More people challenging the rules

"The greatest crimes in the world are not committed by people breaking the rules but by people following the rules," says Banksy, the elusive English street artist and political activist.[58]

Legendary civil rights activist and campaigner John Lewis, a US congressional representative, in 2016, gave a commencement speech to the graduating students of the Massachusetts College of Liberal Arts in which he urged them: "Go out there, get in the way, get in trouble. Good trouble, necessary trouble, and make some noise ..."[59]

This is the concept of "good trouble."

Causing "good trouble" is not breaking the rules for the sake of breaking the rules; it's breaking the rules to replace them with something better.

Be more pirate. The pirate organization breaks the existing codes and creates new ones, which will later be re-appropriated by legitimate governments and organizations.

The book to dig deeper: *Be More Pirate: Or How to Take on the World and Win* by Sam Conniff Allende.[60]

7. More vulnerability

Vulnerability is proof of courage. This is exactly what we demonstrate when we lead, when we take a stand, and when we show up. The courage to be vulnerable is not about winning or losing, it's about the courage to show up when you can't predict or control the outcome.

Without vulnerability, there is no creativity or innovation. Because there is nothing more uncertain than the creative process, and there is no innovation without failure.

"Show me a culture in which vulnerability is framed as weakness and I'll show you a culture struggling to come up with fresh ideas and new perspectives,"

writes Brené Brown, professor of management studies in her book *Dare to Lead.*[61]

As Amy Poehler, the American actress, comedian, and writer said: "It's very hard to have ideas. It's very hard to put yourself out there, it's very hard to be vulnerable, but those people who do that are the dreamers, the thinkers, and the creators. They are the magic people of the world."[62]

The book to dig deeper: *Dare to Lead: Brave Work. Tough Conversations. Whole Hearts* by Brené Brown.

8. A safer place

A safe place is a place in which you can be your true self without fear of judgment. It's a place where you can ask questions, share ideas, be crazy, challenge the status quo and the Overton Window.[63]

It's a place where profit is replaced by purpose and values, it's a place where the hierarchical pyramid is replaced by networks of teams, it's a place where rules and control are replaced by freedom and trust and it's a place where job descriptions are replaced by talent and mastery.

The book to dig deeper: *Corporate Rebels: Make work more fun* by Joost Minnaar and Pim de Morree.[64]

9. More learnings

Are you working at the lab, or the factory? You work at one, or the other.

At the lab, the aim is to find new ways to do things, to find breakthroughs. Failure is embraced as an inevitable consequence of trying to figure out what works and what doesn't.

The factory, on the other hand, wants no surprises. It wants what it did yesterday, but faster and cheaper. It prizes reliability and productivity.

Is your company a lab, in search of the new thing, or a factory, grinding out what's needed today?

"Anyone who says failure is not an option has also ruled out innovation," writes Seth Godin.[65]

Consider a very specific topic ...

... Dig deeper for several hours ...

... And you will know more about it than 99 percent of people, including the ones in your organization.

Learning and knowing is a decision.

Going from a knowing culture (fixed mindset, factory) to a learning culture (growth mindset, lab) with the capacity to experiment and learn, is an essential journey, considering the world is changing faster than ever and uncertainty is growing.

The book to dig deeper: *Black Box Thinking: Why Most People Never Learn from Their Mistakes—But Some Do* by Matthew Syed.[66]

10. More collaboration

Smart organizations know that most skilled people do not work for them. They know that 99.99 percent of the skills they are looking for are outside the boundaries of the organization.

This is why they foster external innovation.

External innovation is about accepting that internal skills and competencies could be advantageously reinforced by external skills and competencies in order to build a specific, perfectly suited response to a defined problem.

It's a posture of humility.

External innovation is a generic term that describes all the possibilities that an organization has for collaborating with third parties to create IP (academics, startups, or corporate).

The book to dig deeper: *Harvesting External Innovation: Managing External Relationships and Intellectual Property* by Donal O'Connell.[67]

A never-ending journey

Creating and nurturing a fearless innovation culture is a never-ending journey. Moving the pawns toward the ten elements described above requires continuous questioning, especially in today's world, which is rapidly changing in sometimes unpredictable directions. There is no recipe and no right or wrong answer; however, putting efforts into these ten elements will improve creativity, agility, and resilience, which are three of the key skills an organization needs to stay relevant through time.

A startup should be seen as a "positive culture pyramid"— Art, Science, and Craft—where Inspiration and Intuition keep abreast with Management and Planning, with PEOPLE at its core. Surrounded by a positive culture that nurtures ideas aimed at your WHY, your core purpose, in the present and the future.

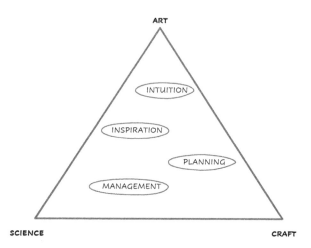

Figure 15: A startup should be seen as a "positive culture pyramid"—Art, Science, and Craft—where Inspiration and Intuition keep abreast with Management and Planning. A positive culture nurtures ideas aimed at your WHY, your core purpose.

Intuition and inner calm allow you to better connect with people. But intuition and inner calm come from wisdom, and your capacity for critical reflection. Unfortunately, wisdom is not something you can communicate. Wisdom is like intelligence. When you try to impart it, it sounds like foolishness to someone else. You can communicate knowledge, but not wisdom. You can find wisdom, live it, work wonders with it, but you cannot communicate and teach it.

Mapping a business model is one thing, implementing it is an entirely different undertaking.

Innovation culture versus corporate culture

Depending on what the organization is about, both can be more or less interpenetrated. Once the innovation culture is in place and it is truly lived by people within the organization, it's potentially interesting to leverage it in the outside world.

Hiut Denim with the publication of a Yearbook[68] and Zappos with their Culture Book[69] are two famous examples of organizations that live their values and culture internally and show them to the world in a way to support the brand.

The cost of not having an innovation culture

The best example of what a lack of innovative culture can cost a company is perhaps in the year 2000, which marked the release of Nokia's 3310 cellphone. At the time, the company was ten times more valuable than Apple. Just how Nokia failed to nail the smartphone market is the quintessential textbook case study even today. One of the research findings from the Åbo Akademi, in Turku, Finland was that Nokia had an indifferent innovation policy.[70] According to the expert opinion of Ben Wood, a technology analyst at CCS Insight, "they were simply not up to the task for innovation. They missed the importance of software."[71]

Many startups are doing what we already know and are not investing in the difficult task of creating something new. As Peter Thiel wrote in his book *Zero to One*, "Other animals are instinctively driven to build things like dams or honeycombs, but we are the only ones that can invent new things and better ways of making them."[72]

Of course, there is no formula to success, but innovation is the closest to a miracle in any business. It undoubtedly lifts the business to new heights. If you look at the big tech companies, you realize that despite the brilliant people who work there, the biggest profits are driven by the culture of innovation that exists within the organization. This innovation culture allows people to be creative. If you want to revolutionize your business offering, the most valuable weaponry in your arsenal would certainly be innovation.

You can make huge profits by leaping into the realm of innovative ingenuity. It also allows you to raise capital for your business strategy. This isn't just talk shop matter. People have turned their fortunes. Innovation can transform the entire value chain of an industry. Essentially, innovation allows you to "crack the code" on how to do business efficiently.

If you are thinking of starting up a company, the future is yours to make. Keep in mind that a company's most important strength is not its size. It is its potential to innovate. Innovative prowess is at the epicenter of a thriving business. You do not have to be a dominant multinational giant, but you certainly need a good dose of innovative brainpower. After all, small does not mean non-existent!

(*Jean-Marie Buchilly, Massimo Scalzo,* and *Aluwani Nemukula*)

CONCLUSION: BY READERS, FOR READERS

This book has been written by a collective of authors who come from different geographical areas and even different continents. In this book, they share their wisdom through the prism of their culture, experience, knowledge, and skills. This is probably what makes the content of this book so unique.

Our inspiration sources are multiple and diverse. Being a reader is a great way to become a writer which explains why some famous authors and their powerful concepts have been leveraged in the book. We tried to connect, combine or expand these concepts to bring added value to the discussion.

Zero to One: Notes on Startups, or How to Build the Future by Peter Thiel, *Start with Why: How Great Leaders Inspire Everyone to Take Action* by Simon Sinek, and *This Is Marketing: You Can't Be Seen Until You Learn to See* by Seth Godin are some of them. Miguel Aubouy, a Canadian French-speaking author and innovator, who has a philosophical approach to innovation, has been our source of inspiration for the three steps that guide us when bringing something new to the world. We encourage you to discover all the books and watch some webinars, talks, or conferences these people hold to dive deeper into their body of work.

Remember that it starts with a key observation (tension), then there is the key idea (assertion), and finally comes the key object (value proposition). This is the backbone of the journey and all the tools, use cases, experiences, and reflections that we share in the book are here to make the whole concrete and tangible; because we all experimented with the full journey through our respective experiences.

Now it's your turn. The only reason why we wrote this book is for you to use as a source of inspiration and a tool to start building your piece of art. The tension that you feel and the assertion you have made to solve it are the reasons why you need to make your voice heard.

You already have this in you, the book is only a toolbox that will help you in structuring, developing, and sharing your worldview, and transforming a concept into a value proposition in the real world.

We encourage you to share your story and the way this book helped you unleash *your* entrepreneurial spirit and make a difference. Send us your story to saumita@letsauthor.com. We'd LOVE to hear about it!

NOTES

1. Peter Thiel, the legendary entrepreneur-investor and the Founder of PayPal, in his book *Zero to One*, elaborates on the importance of building new things, and underlines the fact that today's "best practices" are dead-ends; the best paths are new and untried.

2. In *Do Purpose: Why brands with a purpose do better and matter more*, David Hieatt, often described as a marketing genius, offers insights on how to build one of those purpose-driven companies. You know, those rare brands we all fall in love with.

Introduction

3. A team of researchers from the Medical University of Vienna and Goldsmiths University of London found that lightbulb moments light up dopamine 'factories' in the brain. See https://www.gold.ac.uk/news/aha-moment-dopamine/

I: YOUR BRILLIANT IDEA

Chapter 1: Your Serendipitous Discovery

4. Melanie Parker's story is drawn from two articles. The first one is this CNBC article: How a 32-year-old turned a high school yearbook idea into a $3.2 billion business. https://www.cnbc.com/2020/01/09/canva-how-melanie-perkins-built-a-3point2-billion-dollar-design-start-up.html

5. Canva reaches $15 billion. https://www.forbes.com/sites/alexkonrad/2021/04/06/canva-reaches-15-billion-valuation-making-cofounders-melanie-perkins-and-cliff-obrecht-billionaires

6. Miguel Aubouy, a Canadian French speaking author and innovator, who has sort of a philosophical approach on innovation, has been our source of inspiration for the three steps that guide us when bringing something new to the world.

7. The James Dyson Foundation tells his story quite elegantly. https://www.jamesdysonfoundation.co.uk/who-we-are/our-story.html

Chapter 2: Why This Idea?

8. Simon Sinek's *Start with Why* is perhaps the most elegant and authoritative work on the importance of always remembering your core purpose, cause or belief behind everything you do. Your WHY.

II: THE GROUNDWORK

Chapter 3: Embrace the Uncertainty and Make Better Decisions

9. Inputs taken from this blog on Decision Framing: https://simplicable.com/new/decision-framing

10. Sunk cost is defined as a cost already incurred that is not subject to variation or revision and that is usually represented by a fixed asset purchased and in use. (Source: Merriam-Webster.com Dictionary). Jean-Marie Buchilly, one of the co-authors of this book, is an avid reader who frequently synthesizes his knowledge and insights in the form of blogs. Here is one of his blogs that talks about sunk costs: https://itsyourturnblog.com/sunk-costs-b1e5d3e835b4

11. "Motivational Reasons for Biased Decisions: The Sunk-Cost Effect's Instrumental Rationality." https://www.ncbi.nlm.nih.gov/pmc/articles/PMC5976877/

12. A paper on decision structuring for real-life decision making. https://link.springer.com/article/10.1007/s10677-018-9877-7

13. Katya Andresen is a veteran marketer and nonprofit professional who regularly posts inspiring and insightful articles on LinkedIn. https://www.linkedin.com/pulse/how-avoid-small-frame-pitfall-making-big-decisions-katya-andresen/

14. *A Beautiful Constraint* is a book about everyday, practical inventiveness, designed for the constrained times in which we live.

15. Remembering the mistakes of Challenger. https://www.nasaspaceflight.com/2007/01/remembering-the-mistakes-of-challenger/

16. Another of Jean-Marie's insightful blogs: https://itsyourturnblog.com/safe-2bfe8ae32868

17. A detailed post on the cause of the Space Shuttle Challenger explosion. https://priceonomics.com/the-space-shuttle-challenger-explosion-and-the-o/

18. https://seths.blog/2020/04/all-models-are-wrong-some-models-are-useful/

19. *Creating Great Choices* is a how-to book on moving beyond trade-off thinking and create a new and superior answer, also see https://itsyourturnblog.com/decision-making-creating-great-choices-through-iterative-thinking-19dd2b4b129

20. The term "tension" used here, and at various places throughout this book, refers to the tension that is created from opposing models or ideas. Roger L. Martin, in his article "How Successful Readers Think" published in Harvard Business Review, writes: "We were born with opposable minds, which allow us to hold two conflicting ideas in constructive, almost dialectic tension. We can use that tension to think our way toward new, superior ideas." Anything that changes the status quo is also creating tension. https://hbr.org/2007/06/how-successful-leaders-think

21. A thought-provoking blog on shared objective reality. https://seths.blog/2020/03/shared-objective-reality/

22. Critical thinking, with its roots in the mid-late 20th century, is a rich concept that has been developing throughout the past 2,500 years. In philosophical terms, it is the awakening of the intellect to the study of itself. https://www.criticalthinking.org/pages/defining-critical-thinking/766

23. Simon Bradley and Nicole Price wrote a short and powerful book on Critical Thinking, that's definitely worth a read if you're interested in this topic: *Critical Thinking: Proven Strategies To Improve Decision Making Skills, Increase Intuition And Think Smarter*

24. A superb book if you want to embrace uncertainty and make better decisions: *Thinking in Bets*.

25. In this witty TED talk, neuroscientist Stuart Firestein gets to the heart of science as it is really practiced and suggests that we should value what we don't know—or "high-quality ignorance"—just as much as what we know. https://www.ted.com/talks/stuart_firestein_the_pursuit_of_ignorance

26. An article summarizing the book *Thinking in Bets*, written by Jean-Marie

Buchilly. The main idea is that "Great decisions don't always lead to great outcomes, bad decisions don't always lead to bad outcomes."

27. Why do we make illogical decisions all the time? In *Predictably Irrational* Dan Ariely cuts to the heart of our strange behaviours.

28. The central idea behind the book *10-10-10: A Life-Transforming Idea* by Suzy Welch, is the following. When you're facing a dilemma, all it takes to begin are three questions: What are the consequences of my decision in 10 minutes? In 10 months? And in 10 years? Exploring the impact of our decisions in multiple time frames surfaces our unconscious agendas, fears, needs, and desires, and ultimately helps us identify and live according to our deepest goals and values.

29. The article on *Thinking in Bets* as above. https://itsyourturnblog.com/decision-making-thinking-in-bets-5863a16fb92f

30. An article summarizing of Brené Brown's book *Dare to Lead.* https://buchilly.medium.com/the-man-in-the-arena-a52098b31d2e

31. An excerpt from the speech "Citizenship In A Republic" delivered by Theodore Roosevelt at the Sorbonne, in Paris, France on April 23, 1910. https://www.theodorerooseveltcenter.org/Learn-About-TR/TR-Encyclopedia/Culture-and-Society/Man-in-the-Arena.aspx

Chapter 4: Giving Legs to Your Ideas

32. Inspiring success story of Ingvar Kamprad, founder of IKEA. http://inspireminds.in/englishblog/1028/inspiring-success-story-of-ingvar-kamprad-founder-of-ikea.html

33. The Blue Ocean Strategy, a term first proposed by Chan Kim & Renée Mauborgne in their classic book by the same name, is about creating and capturing uncontested market space, thereby making the competition irrelevant. It is the simultaneous pursuit of differentiation and low cost to open up a new market space and create new demand. https://www.blueoceanstrategy.com/what-is-blue-ocean-strategy/

Chapter 5: Understand Your Customer: Status, Worldviews, Beliefs

34. *Swim with the Sharks Without Being Eaten Alive: Outsell, Outmanage, Outmotivate, and Outnegotiate Your Competition* by Harvey Mackay.

35. An MVP or Minimum Viable Product is a version of a new product which allows collecting maximum amount of learnings about customers with the least amount of effort and minimum development time.

36. This quote is from a powerful book that's all about customer empathy: *Meaningful: The Story of Ideas That Fly* by Bernadette Jiwa

37. Seth Godin's first and very unique book on leadership: *Tribes: We need you to lead us.*

Chapter 6: Why Wait? Go Fund Yourself

38. Ash Maurya, in his book *Running Lean* explains bootstrapping. He writes, "bootstrapping is more commonly understood as a collection of techniques used to minimize the amount of external debt or funding needed from banks or investors. Too often, people confuse bootstrapping with self-funding. A stricter definition is funding with customer revenues."

39. Software as a service, or SaaS, is a software licensing and delivery model in which software is licensed on a subscription basis and is centrally hosted.

Chapter 7: Do You Need a Co-founder

40. The Slicing Pie is a universal, one-size-fits all model to create a fair equity split in an early-stage, bootstrapped startup company. https://slicingpie.com/

III: STEP INTO THE ARENA

Chapter 8: The Innovator's Model

41. Susanna Nissar runs the Social Innovation Booster program, and describes a "User Centered Innovation Loop" inspired by Design Thinking. https://www.innovationbooster.org/post/user-centered-innovation-loop

42. *The Lean Startup: How Constant Innovation Creates Radically Successful Businesses* by Eric Ries is a ground-breaking book on thinking lean in the context of startups. It is a popular approach to business that's being adopted around the world. It is changing the way companies are built and new products are launched.

43. "How DropBox Started As A Minimal Viable Product." https://techcrunch.com/2011/10/19/dropbox-minimal-viable-product/

44. A/B testing, at its most basic, is a way to compare two versions of something to figure out which performs better. While it's most often associated with websites and apps, the method is almost 100 years old. https://hbr.org/2017/06/a-refresher-on-ab-testing

Chapter 9: The Innovator's Canvas

45. A business model is nothing else than a representation of how an organization makes (or intends to make) money. Entrepreneurs want to find new and innovative business models to carve out their space in the marketplace. Business models help entrepreneurs increase their capacity to manage continuous change and constantly adapt to rapidly changing business environments by injecting new ideas into their business model. http://businessmodelalchemist.com/2005/11/what-is-business-model.html

46. Lean Canvas is a 1-page business plan template created by Ash Maurya, optimized for the Lean Startup methodology with a big emphasis on finding customer problems worth solving. https://leanstack.com/is-one-page-business-model

47. Seth Godin offers the core of his marketing wisdom in *This is Marketing: You Can't Be Seen Until You Learn To See*. Read it for the insights it offers into how, and why, we buy things or change our habits in any way.

IV: SHOW YOURSELF

Chapter 10: Tell Your Story, Share Your Assertions, Get Their Attention

48. You're either remarkable or invisible. Make your choice. Urges Seth Godin in his book *Purple Cow*.

49. In *Traction: How Any Startup Can Achieve Explosive Customer Growth*, serial entrepreneurs Gabriel Weinberg and Justin Mares give startups the tools for generating explosive customer growth.

Chapter 11: Branding and Brand Marketing

50. This epic trilogy traverses parallel universes with witches, armored polar bears, and daemons. https://www.philip-pullman.com/hdm

Chapter 12: Create Valuable Intellectual Property

51 An interesting article on IP risk management. Covers topics such as: Where do intellectual property risks originate from? How do you set up an effective IP Management? https://www.ipeg.com/ip-risk-management-how-to-deal-with-it-part-1

Chapter 15: Fearless Innovation

52. If you are from a new breed of social activists working within, about to join or completely disillusioned by today's business world - to be the change you want to see in your company, *The Intrapreneur: Confessions of a corporate insurgent* by Gib Bulloch is the book for you. We are in the age of the intrapreneur: where mavericks and rebels bring their entrepreneurial prowess to big business, to change it from the inside out and bottom up.

53. Seth Godin regularly blogs. His blogs are inspiring and teach how to level up. The statement mentioned here comes from one of his older blogs titled *Reject the tyranny of being picked: pick yourself*. https://seths. blog/2011/03/reject-the-tyranny-of-being-picked-pick-yourself/

54. In *Extreme Ownership (How U.S. Navy SEALs Lead and Win)*, two U.S. Navy SEAL officers, Jocko Willink and Leif Babin, who led the most highly decorated special operations unit of the Iraq War, demonstrate how to apply powerful leadership principles from the battlefield to business and life.

55. We have been taught that success in any field requires early specialization and many hours of deliberate practice. In *Range: Why Generalists Triumph in a Specialized World*, David Epstein shows you that the way to succeed is by sampling widely, gaining a breadth of experiences, taking detours, experimenting relentlessly, juggling many interests—in other words, by developing range.

56. In *The Coaching Habit: Say Less, Ask More & Change the Way You Lead Forever*, Michael Bungay Stanier unpacks seven essential coaching questions to demonstrate how-by saying less and asking more-you can develop coaching methods that produce great results.

57. First published in 1989, *Leadership Is an Art* by Max De Pree has long been a must-read not only within the business community but also in professions ranging from academia to medical practices, to the political arena.

58. Banksy, Britain's now-legendary "guerilla" street artist, has painted the walls, streets, and bridges of towns and cities throughout the world. Not only did he smuggle his pieces into four of New York City's major art museums, he's also "hung" his work at London's Tate Gallery and adorned Israel's West Bank barrier with satirical images. Banksy's identity remains unknown, but his work is unmistakable with prints selling for as

much as $45,000. The quote mentioned is from *Wall and Piece*, a photo compilation of Banksy's works.

59. Rep. John Lewis, a congressman from Georgia with a long history in civil rights activism and leadership, tells a packed house of hopeful graduates at the Massachusetts College of Liberal Arts, to go and change the world, get in the way, get in trouble, necessary trouble, and make some noise. https://www.berkshireeagle.com/archives/rep-john-lewis-get-in-necessary-trouble/article_b57373b3-6991-588f-8f6b-2aa413a521f8.html

60 In *Be More Pirate: Or How to Take on the World and Win*, Sam Conniff Allende unveils the innovative strategies of Golden Age pirates, drawing parallels between the tactics and teachings of legends like Henry Morgan and Blackbeard with modern rebels, like Elon Musk, Malala and Banksy.

61 Leaders are people who hold themselves accountable for recognizing the potential in people and ideas, and developing that potential. *Dare to Lead: Brave Work. Tough Conversations. Whole Hearts* by Brené Brown is a book for everyone who is ready to choose courage over comfort, make a difference and lead.

62 In Amy Poehler's book *Yes Please*, she offers a juicy stew of personal stories, funny bits on love and friendship and parenthood, and real-life advice. *Yes Please* is a book full of words to live by.

63 The Overton Window is a model for understanding how ideas in society change over time and influence politics. The core concept is that politicians are limited in what policy ideas they can support— they generally only pursue policies that are widely accepted throughout society as legitimate policy options. These policies lie inside the Overton Window. https://www.mackinac.org/OvertonWindow

64. *Corporate Rebels: Make work more fun* by Joost Minnaar and Pim de Morree is written for people who know workplaces could, and should, be better.

65. In his blog "The lab or the factory," Seth Godin eloquently differentiates between a working environment that operates as a lab, wholeheartedly accepting failure as the cost of generating insights, versus a factory where efficiency is prized.

66. *Black Box Thinking: Why Most People Never Learn from Their Mistakes—But Some Do* by Matthew Syed. A definite read for everyone more than twice to inculcate the way of growth mindset who makes failures as friends and difficulties as opportunities to learn.

67. *Harvesting External Innovation*, a book by Donal O'Connell, one of the co-authors of this book, addresses the growing phenomenon of external

innovation, where companies are cooperating and collaborating with a variety of external parties, driven by a passion for innovation.

68. People at Hiut Denim believe that there is a great deal of satisfaction to be gained from making something well, of such superior quality that you know it is going to stand the test of time. It makes the hard work and the obsessing over each and every detail worth all the effort. Through their yearbooks, they let the world know more about their ways and beliefs. https://hiutdenim.co.uk/collections/yearbook-5

69. The Zappos Culture Book. https://www.zapposinsights.com/culture-book/digital-version

70. In a 2014 paper *How Nokia Failed to Nail the Smartphone Market*, a group of Finnish researchers discuss Nokia's struggle to find a sustainable approach to the Smartphone market. www.econstor.eu/bitstream/10419/101414/1/794346243.pdf

71. A BBC article on the rise and fall of Nokia. https://www.bbc.com/news/technology-23947212

72. Peter Thiel elaborates on the importance of creating something new, and not merely copying others in this ground-breaking and thought-provoking book on innovation: *Zero to One*.

ABOUT THE AUTHORS

Saumita Banerjee
India

Saumita is an entrepreneur and technology enthusiast. She started LetsAuthor in 2019, initiating a new era in the world of writing books. During her eight-year stint at NineSigma, she gained insights into Open Innovation and got to meet a number of entrepreneurs who were making change happen. These experiences collectively inspired her to enter the entrepreneurial world, adapt the practice of Open Innovation into an unrelated area of book writing, and introduce the concept of Open Authoring. This book is a proof-of-concept project for her to demonstrate that Open Authoring works and to illustrate the magic of smartly utilizing the collective wisdom of intellectuals. For this book, she's worn multiple hats: apart from leading the writing of this book, she coordinated all activities that made this book happen: positioning, structuring and re-structuring, coordinating co-author contributions, publishing, marketing, and so on. She actively practices the ideas and knowledge shared in this book to grow her venture.

Jean-Marie Buchilly
Switzerland

Jean-Marie is an ideas connector and a compulsive reader. He regularly writes posts on Medium in order to share his worldview, his thoughts and some actionable summaries of the books he reads and he is now actively working on his own book that will combine two of his passions: wine and innovation. He is in charge of innovation for an international organization since 2018 and he has also developed the participative innovation program for this same company in 2017. He started building innovation within the organization from scratch right after having attended altMBA by Seth Godin in 2016, a truly inspiring and transformational online course that showed him a powerful way to make change happen. Along this intrapreneurial journey, he had to face multiple challenges and found great help in multiple books written by those who were either sharing their methodologies or their experiences. The book you hold in your hands is an opportunity for him to share his own experience and learnings while experimenting the unique experience of open collaboration in the field of authoring. He strongly believes that a group of highly motivated people can achieve almost everything and the publication of this book tends to prove him right.

Yehoshua Zlotogorski
Israel

Yehoshua is an entrepreneur based in Israel. He co-founded Alpe Audio, a new kind of audio platform, that is changing the way we learn. Learning is a lifelong endeavor of discovery, curiosity, self, and career improvement. In today's on-the-go lifestyle, Alpe offers educational content tailored for learners "on-the-go": while commuting, running errands, or out for a jog. Alpe's courses are built together with leading industry experts and academia and incorporate proven cognitive learning techniques. In this book, Yehoshua shares his experience bootstrapping user growth at Alpe from zero to 10,000 users.

Simon Krystman
United Kingdom

Simon Krystman is a serial entrepreneur and startup mentor🚀. He has founded many startups over the last three decades, mainly in the tech space. Recently his focus has been on mentorship and philanthropy, through crowdfunding and his involvement with 12Ronnies, who help novice founders launch startups. This book is important to Simon in a number of ways: crowdsourcing, co-creation and knowledge sharing is fundamental to the future he is playing a part in developing. His Customer Launch Philosophy is at the heart of his vision for an ideas economy that drives humanity across the Rubicon from an information age to a golden age of ideas.

Shyjal Raazi
India

Shyjal Raazi is a serial entrepreneur. He bootstrapped a fully remote SaaS startup along with his co-founder Aslam Abbas. He used to attend several hackathons and startup events since college and was a consultant for few startups. These experiences collectively inspired him to build a product named Collect.chat in 2017. Collect.chat got good traction and is now being used by around 25,000 businesses all around the world. Shyjal firmly believes in the concept of collective wisdom embodied in this book. Through this book, he shares his knowledge and hopes to learn from other entrepreneurs while growing his startup.

Aluwani Nemukula
South Africa

Aluwani Nemukula is a scientist turned agripreneur. He epitomizes the ideal modern farmer: versatile, curious and tech-savvy— most importantly he is on a quest to bringing affordable vegetables to every household in South Africa. Setting up hydroponics structures in his research lab, that eventually yielded him bumper crops such as sweet peppers and butter lettuce, was the ultimate drawcard for this self-taught and ambitious farmer. He saw the gap in local fresh produce markets and decided to use his innovative skills to change the agricultural landscape and productivity in Africa. At the heart of Aluwani's farming operations is the technology-oriented portable grower—VegiGrower™—that combines organic farming with convenience. He shares some of his startup experience in this book, detailing his journey on how to enter and succeed in some difficult-to-crack markets. Born and bred in the Limpopo Province of South Africa, Aluwani shares tips on how to overcome startup challenges by using innovation to differentiate your business offering. His business advice: "start small and grow bigger." While managing his farming operations, he still finds time to lecture university students and mentor aspiring farmers on a consultancy basis.

Aditya Bhatnagar
France

Aditya Bhatnagar is an entrepreneur and strategist. He strategized and supported more than ten businesses within six months during Covid times. With six plus years of working experience in multiple industries including banking, education, health & fitness, technology, and retail, he has supported students, pre-launch founders (across Europe and UK) to develop understanding of business, innovation, management, and marketing. With an educational background of engineering, banking, marketing, and management he gives a broader-to-niches approach to businesses. Two-times awarded for his targeted results toward the business, he brings insightful strategy and actions on the table. With this book, he shares the approaches and solutions pre-launch founders should know while they go through the journey from idea to launch. This book is special not only because of the topic but because it takes him to being an author practicing the skill of writing and as he says a skill each one of us should practice. Collaborating with other leaders and entrepreneurs from different domains brings fresh perspective which was a big learning experience. This book is testament to the many cases and failures he faced throughout his journey mixed with education and entrepreneurial experiences.

Susanna Nissar
Sweden

Susanna Nissar is an entrepreneur, service and business designer and customer experience enthusiast. She is the founder of Social Innovation Booster, a global community and learning platform for people who are using their entrepreneurial skills for social innovation.

Susanna was an early adopter of design thinking in Sweden, and co-founded the service design agency Expedition Mondial. For more than ten years, she worked as a service and business design consultant with clients in the public sector. The goal for these organizations is to design public services that citizens value and trust. Social Innovation Booster was founded to democratize the access to these human-centered innovation tools so that impact-oriented entrepreneurs knew how to create great customer experiences and successful services. By participating in this open authoring book Susanna hopes to spread the human-centered approach to a wider audience. And it was a lot of fun to participate too!

Christopher Norris
United Kingdom

Christopher Norris is an entrepreneur and publishing expert. He pioneered World Book Day in the UK in the mid-1990s and popularizes the Icelandic "Christmas book flood" tradition, Jolabokaflodid. He is also a director at 12Ronnies, co-founder of the Founders and Mentors platform for pre-launch founders and creatives, and co-founder of CrowdMall, which validates ideas in the marketplace via pre-sales. His career spans an increasing scope of influence: from qualified schoolteacher, through editor of countless books, to digital strategist on a global scale. This book project was hosted at CrowdMall when the site launched in March 2021; Christopher was keen to contribute to this LetsAuthor launch title in return. He is a keen advocate of disruptive technologies for the common good, a theme that is a seam that runs through his career in the arts, media and business sectors.

Donal O'Connell
United Kingdom

Donal O' Connell is the Managing Director of Chawton Innovation Services. His company offers consultancy in the areas of innovation and intellectual property management. Put simply, his company helps clients to appreciate their intellectual capital, assets and property, and to ensure that they then manage these intangibles in an efficient and effective manner. His client base includes multi-nationals, SMEs, legal & IP firms, financial services entities as well as universities. He graduated from NIHE Limerick (now The University of Limerick) in Ireland in 1985, with a degree in electronic engineering. Formerly a VP of R&D and a Director of IP at Nokia, he has had a long career at Nokia for twenty-one years and has wide and varied experience in the wireless telecoms industry, having worked for periods in The Netherlands, UK, USA, Finland, and HK. He is a Visiting Researcher at Imperial College Business School in London, and teaches about "IP management." His first book *Inside the Patent Factory* was published by Wiley & Sons in 2008. His second book *Harvesting External Innovation* was published by Gower Publishing in mid-2011. He has also written a large number of papers on various aspects of innovation and IP which have been published in a number of magazines, websites and blogs around the world. Since 2013, he has been included into the IAM 300 (the world's leading IP strategists) an annual listing of those individuals identified as offering operating companies and other IP owners' world-class advice on maximizing the value of their intellectual property. Together with some associates, he also coaches and mentors startup companies on innovation and entrepreneurship.

Massimo Scalzo
Germany

Massimo Scalzo is an entrepreneur, mentor, sportsman, humanist, traveler, storyteller. Someone who made a business dream come true, for himself and others, and helps people do the same. For nearly twenty-eight years Massimo traveled and worked in management consulting in eight countries. His thoughts, notions, ideas, projects and programs and speaking engagements come from more than thirteen years as an entrepreneur in which he started a CRM consulting company, among others, that very quickly grew so much to being bought out by a global giant of Information Technology. Before becoming an entrepreneur, he spent fourteen plus years "on the road" for Touche & Ross, Deloitte, and PricewaterHouse. On his path, he learned a great deal about humanized leadership, customer-driven strategy and transformation, digital marketing and design thinking, working on behalf of a-z roster of clients, e.g., IBM, BMW, Frost & Sullivan, SAP, Oracle, Fiat Group, Salesforce, Accenture, OpenMinds and many other companies in several countries and industries. He adds a few personal words about LetsAuthor, "I think what LetsAuthor is doing is admirable and necessary. This book is proof of that. We need another breed of leaders and entrepreneurs in the world - to do so we need knowledge, experience and people who can inspire and instill a sense of beauty and creativity in other people who want to jump into the magic of entrepreneurship. That's why I decided to make my humble contribution to the drafting of this book. My small contribution is like passing the baton to young people who, like me years ago, are chasing a dream. Thank you LetsAuthor!"

Meenakshi Babu
India

Meenakshi Babu is a lucid realist and a positive enthusiast. She has a master's in innovation and entrepreneurship from HEC Paris. Her passion for innovation has furthered her deep investment in crafting solutions that go beyond pre-built frontiers and has steered her to social entrepreneurship. She founded the Yugen Education Foundation to transform the rural education system through scalable training solutions for the school adult community. She also has a master's in education and has over seventeen years of experience as an educator, including teaching at business schools. She is endlessly fascinated by the human ability to learn, adapt, and change and lives by the motto, "quality learning for all." She is a Stanford d.school certified design thinker and has built her work on the principles of design thinking. Apart from teaching, she is also a strategy and innovation consultant and trains aspiring entrepreneurs. The LetsAuthor platform was a natural extension of her work to reach out to budding entrepreneurs. Her participation in creating this book shows her appreciation of the idea of crowdsourcing expert knowledge and her belief that life is about shared belonging.

Ilanit Appelfeld
Israel

Ilanit Appelfeld is an intellectual property attorney, based in Israel. She helps companies protect their competitive advantage through patents, trade secrets, designs and trade-marks. She loves working with her clients' teams to get patents registered, but she also knows that patents are not the only tool in the IP toolbox. After years of working with companies in different industries, she has discovered the right path for companies to protect and capitalize on their gold. In this book, she shares her knowledge and wisdom on how companies can protect and communicate their value effectively, using the right tools.

Susanna Schumacher
Sweden

Susanna Schumacher is an entrepreneurial fountain of ideas. She has worked professionally with business development and is always eager to find ways to collaborate, develop, and make change with others. During her first year of studying social entrepreneurship, she also started her first company, and has ever since been interested in finding ways to share her experience and knowledge from this journey. The opportunity to collaborate with other like-minded people, and the desire to grow a seed of her lifetime dream to become an author were her way in to contribute to this book.

Suraj Rajan
India

Suraj Rajan is an entrepreneur and a product design consultant. He has years of experience in product development in automobile ancillary, medical and safety products domains. He co-founded Faberz Technologies in 2016, helping companies design their service model and new product development strategies, while ensuring operational and technological efficiency to support the growth of the business.

ABOUT THE LETSAUTHOR COMMUNITY

At LetsAuthor, we are building a community of experts and professionals to come together and write books on a variety of topics. We believe that each one of us has a unique story to tell, an experience to share, and we are giving you the opportunity to be heard, to make a difference. We follow the philosophy of Open Authoring. We open each of our books to everyone who wants to participate. We choose the contributions that are most valuable to our readers, carefully validate the content, weave a beautiful story that our readers will love, and present a brand-new book to the world, one at a time!

If you too have a story or an experience to share and would like to become a part of our author community, please visit https://letsauthor.com/ and sign up as a Lead Author or a Contributor. Please let us know the areas you would like to contribute, and we will consider opening a new book if one isn't already in the making.

https://letsauthor.com/

OUR EARLY BACKERS

A BIG THANK YOU to our early backers, who believed enough in *In the Arena* and LetsAuthor to pre-order a copy, when it was merely a landing page.

— Co-Authors, *In the Arena*

Tim Strege
Cresti Barbara
Marlène Henry Lendi
Massimiliano Freddi
Tomas Conefrey
Lynette Kontny
Olivier Chappuis
Stephen Clulow
John Speyrer
Patrizio Bortolus
Benoit Ellenrieder
Geraud de Laval
Kiran Kadekoppa
Lisa Jane Perraud
Nitin Bahuguna
Subhajit Mukherjee

ILLUSTRATING THE UNIVERSAL INNOVATION PROCESS

Before William Painter invented the crown bottle cap in 1892, there was a persistent problem with stoppers and bottle caps.

Bottled carbonated beverages were already popular by the 1880s, but they lacked reliability. Their caps did not seal the bottle sufficiently, causing liquids and carbonated gases to frequently spill out.[*]

THE KEY OBSERVATION

HOW TO FILL A HOL

THE KE

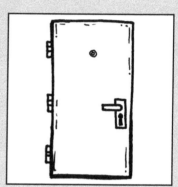

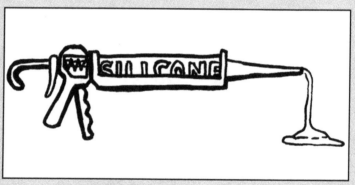

OR, SEAL A BOTTLE)?

DEAS

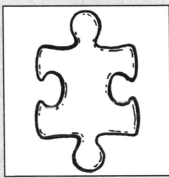

Painter invented the Crown Cork bottle cap with a corrugated-flange edge. To seal the bottle and prevent contact between the metal cap and the drink, he lined it with a thin cork disc and a special paper backing. The solution was simple, economical to produce, and leakproof.

Painter worked with bottling manufacturers to develop a universal neck. He patented all the machinery needed to manufacture the caps. In 1892, he launched the Crown Cork and Seal Company to manufacture and market the cap.

THE KEY OBJECT

With technological advancements, the crown cap has been refined. PVC material replaced the cork disc, the skirt's height was shortened, and the cap's teeth reduced from 24 to 21.

The crown cap is the universal cap used for carbonated beverages in glass bottles even today.

CPSIA information can be obtained
at www.ICGtesting.com
Printed in the USA
BVHW032002160921
616745BV00013B/102